"Yet again Karen has wr
easy to read and absorb. V
is for solopreneurs who need
and their business to find a way of breaking
the competition and stand out from the crowd. The
activities and ideas will enable you to consider your
own path to business success in a way which suits you
and your clients. We all need support, guidance and
ideas from time to time and this book will certainly give
you those. Karen's clear instructions mean you could
easily implement her ideas into your own business
starting from NOW."
– **Rebecca Jones,** The Red Shoe Biz Woman,
Enterpise Mentor, Author, Trainer and Professional
Speaker

"Karen Williams has done it again and written a
must-read for all those starting out in business. How
To Stand Out In Your Business is the book I wish I
could buy for every client! Grounded, inspirational and
real with 7 practical steps on how to do everything
from deal with 'fraud syndrome' to win lots of awards,
this is a book that will hold your hand as you create
BIG success in your business."
– **Suzy Greaves,** author of *Making The Big Leap*
and founder of The Big Leap Coaching Company

"How To Stand Out In Your Business is an invaluable
resource, not only for new businesses, but also for those
businesses already established who wish to stand out
and shine even more. Karen has laid the book out in
such a way that it can be followed through strategically
from the beginning, with exercises to work through,
covering your mindset and the practicalities of getting
started and standing out. I will recommend this book
to my own clients who are either beginning their

journey or wishing to step up their business. Thank you, Karen for sharing your experience and knowledge to reach out to others."
> – **Tarryn Hunt,** author of *365 Quotes for Mums That Care,* founder of Mums That Care

"A thoroughly engaging read packed with useful advice and tips based on Karen's own experience. This second book is an excellent follow-on to her first book, refreshing the key steps in her SUCCESS strategy, but expanding them with even more practical strategies to help readers develop a successful service business. Having read it from cover to cover I will go back and study each chapter in more detail and complete the useful exercises to ground these ideas into improved business practice. The book has motivated me to tackle my fears and procrastination and take my coaching business to another level."
> – **Dr Judith Sunley,** Judith Sunley Coaching

"From start to finish, Karen fills you with the excitement of creating your own business; you want to read on and devour all the secrets of success. This book is both inspiring and practical, showing you how to make a difference in the world whilst addressing the reality that we also need to earn a living – a perfect balance. Karen provides a wealth of options for handling the challenges, both psychological and practical. You'll learn from Karen's own ups and downs and the experience of numerous successful and authentic business people she has modelled. Systematically, she guides you through the steps to creating the business you desire and stimulates the belief that it really is possible for you."
> – **Caroline Talbott,** author of *Essential Career Transition Coaching Skills,* Caroline Talbott Limited

How To Stand Out In Your Business

Your Business

The 7 Steps To Success

Karen Williams

ISBN 978 1 849143 09 7

British Library Cataloguing in Publications Data
A catalogue record for this book is available from the British Library

Typeset in Verdana by Shore Books and Design,
Blackborough End, Norfolk PE32 1SF

Printed in Great Britain by Lightning Source UK Ltd
Milton Keynes MK11 3LW

'The journey of a thousand miles begins with a single step'
– Lao Tzu.

Step up, stand out and enjoy the view!

Contents

Foreword

If your business is about helping others then please take this moment to 'punch the air' – for you are one of the new breed of entrepreneurs perfectly positioned to achieve great success in this wonderful new era of the 'Thought Leader'.

I firmly believe that the future of business is not in manufacturing or creating more physical stuff (the last thing the world needs is more stuff); it is about helping others on their journey to personal success and fulfilment. What's more, it's so hugely satisfying to be at the heart of a business where you are serving others by delivering inspiration, happiness, support and wisdom on a daily basis.

In this book Karen Williams has created an essential template covering all the areas you need to know to create a successful, profitable, thriving coaching business. It's a book I wish I had read when I started out as a Business Coach and Mentor many years ago!

I was fortunate in that my entire coaching business landed in my lap – thanks to my lucky break, starring in the first two series of BBC TV's Dragons' Den. Hundreds of (paid) speaking engagements were offered to me (luckily Karen talks about that dread of public speaking which had – and still has - me in its fearful grip before many an engagement), followed by hundreds of people asking for my help with their business.

I ended up shaping a whole range of coaching

products and services based on demand – and had to learn as I went along that the secret of being a good coach does not lie in trying to tell people what to do!

Most coaches do it the other way round – they start out with the training, skills and expertise and then need to go out and market themselves. Karen has described perfectly the keys to becoming a trusted guide within your niche, how to stand out from the crowd and ultimately how to get 'famous' for what you do.

I'm also pleased that Karen has tackled the old thorny issue that comes up for so many people whose business is about helping others, and that is 'Am I good enough?'. Over the years, I've mentored Sales Coaches whose own profits were failing, Healers who had fallen into ill health, Relationship Coaches going through hideous divorces and one particularly memorable 'Happiness Coach' who always used to start each call by telling me how depressed she was.

I remember the sage advice of another coach who told me (in a moment of my own insecurity about my ability to deliver business advice having failed so spectacularly with my first business) 'You only ever need to be a fingernail ahead of someone else to be able to help them.' Robust vulnerability can indeed be an asset when it comes to marketing yourself. You too have known the horrors that life can throw along the way.

My own rollercoaster experience of Business Mentoring is that being a 'people helper' is a far more fulfilling way to spend your life than running a business which is based purely on peddling material 'stuff' - and I wouldn't swap my life now for my previous one, even in the years when I was generating £1million profit a year.

Living a life of success and prosperity is about so much more than just making money.

Luckily, this book will show you not only how to have great fun and fulfilment as a business owner; you'll also discover how to get into flow and create abundance too!

– Rachel Elnaugh
Entrepreneur, star of BBC TV's Dragons' Den, Business Speaker and Author, Mentor and Transformational Coach
www.rachelelnaugh.com

Acknowledgements

The philosophy behind this book is that to stand out in your business, you can't do it alone. You need an 'A' team to motivate you, chivvy you up and support you to achieve success; a principle that I have followed whilst writing this book. It is hard to acknowledge everyone who has helped me to take my business to the next level and complete my second book, so here goes.

Firstly, I would like to thank everyone who has influenced and inspired me over the last few years – you know who you are. I wish to acknowledge the 24 coaches who I interviewed for my first book, *The Secrets of Successful Coaches,* (and subsequent telesummit) whose advice and knowledge turned my business around. It is also important to mention the amazing speakers who are sharing the stage with me at the very first Star Biz conference.

Secondly, it would not have been possible for me to write this book without implementing a system that works; my recognition goes to Lucy Whittington from *Being a Business Celebrity* who helped me to nail my thing and develop my signature system. She enabled me to create a process that I was able to fine-tune to get great results with my clients. In addition, Sheryl Andrews from *Step by Step Listening* who used, (mostly), clean language to help me to realise that I've been using my system effectively for many years with my clients.

Thirdly, and equally important are my clients who have allowed me to experiment, learn from them, and work with them to achieve great results with their businesses.

I would not be here today if it weren't for my right hand woman, friend and virtual assistant, Tracy Harris, and the rest of my support team who join me as I take new leaps, create exciting activities, and deliver amazing events. I wish to acknowledge Christina Harkness, my copy editor, for her support and advice and for assisting me with both of my books.

Of course, nothing would happen without my home support network. My thanks go to Peter for letting me get on with it and believing in me and to my Mum and Dad, Barbara and Ken Legg, who are always there for me and inspire me to make big things happen, even when things aren't going to plan in their own lives.

Lastly, thank you for taking the time to buy and read this book. I look forward to finding out more about your own actions and adventures as you discover how to stand out in your business and shine.

You can contact me at:

- www.HowToStandOut.co.uk

- follow me on Twitter as @selfdiscovery or

- like my Facebook page at www.facebook.com/selfdiscoverycoaching.

Chapter 1
Introduction

'The ladder of success is best climbed by stepping on the rungs of opportunity.' – Ayn Rand

There are many people doing what you do in business. Well, at least a version of what you do. Whether you are a coach, beauty therapist, social media expert or business consultant, you will have competition – other people who believe that they can help your clients to be successful. To capture your client's attention and be their number one choice, you need to learn **how** you can stand out in your business.

It is not enough to be the best in your profession. You need to learn what makes you different, why people should hire you and to make your message clear. You need to know who you can help, where you can find them, and then tell them about the transformations that you provide.

It is not enough to be good at the business side of running a business. You need to know what sets you apart from everyone else, how you can be an expert and how you can employ other experts to make your business work.

It is not enough to launch yourself into the marketplace without knowing what you want. You will need the right strategies to be clear and focused if you are to achieve success.

It is not enough to believe that you are confident

enough to wing it and get the results you want. You need to have the mindset to pick yourself up when things don't go to plan, and motivate yourself when all you want to do is stay in bed.

What happens if you are mediocre, average or just OK? What happens if you play it small? I see many coaches, consultants, and other business owners do this; they remain the world's best kept secret, but what happens then? They don't make it in business, so they struggle, go back to a day job, or do something different to bring in an income.

Over the years, I've noticed many small business owners who struggle to stand out – many not for the want of trying. They don't know how to stand out from the crowd, be different and step into their greatness. They follow the majority rather than what actually works. Then they realise that they can't do the things that they wanted to do when they started in business, so they decide that it's not for them.

We all know the statistics: 20% of business owners get 80% of the clients, and business success is 20% effort and 80% mindset and psychology. With this in mind, you can't be the same as everyone else if you want to achieve success in business.

This is what started me off on my journey. I started my business in 2006 and I was a great coach, but not a very good business owner. My business ticked over for a few years and then, in 2009, I knew that I had to do something drastic to be able to warrant working full time on my business. I realised that it wasn't just me who was struggling. I noticed that a lot of coaches and other business owners were achieving mediocre success in their business. At that time, as part of my NLP Master Practitioner course, I took the opportunity to model the mindset behind a successful coaching business. I initially spent time with 11 successful coaches, those of whom were not only great in their profession, but good in business too. I learnt their secrets and their strategies and applied them to my own business – and they worked – and then I wrote a book about it.

The Secrets of Successful Coaches was launched in 2010, and I went on to interview 13 more successful coaches. During this process, I identified what worked and developed my own SUCCESS system, with help from a mentor who enabled me to see what was at the end of my nose. I applied the techniques to my own business and then shared these strategies with my clients. Strangely enough, I realised later that the process I am sharing with you is one that I have used unwittingly throughout the development of my business. Yet once I gave the process some structure, I discovered the beauty of the system as a whole and the value of the individual parts.

The philosophy behind the system is that to be successful in business, you need to learn how to stand out. You need to learn how to be one of the 20-percenters to help the clients who inspired you to set up your business in the first place.

What needs to happen for you to stand out as a star in your business and learn how to shine?

I'm reminded of a famous quote by Marianne Williamson. It starts like this: 'Our deepest fear is not that we are inadequate. Our deepest fear is that we are powerful beyond measure. It is our light, not our darkness that most frightens us. We ask ourselves, who am I to be brilliant, gorgeous, talented, fabulous? Actually, who are you *not* to be? ...'

Who are you not to be? Frankly, unless you stand out in your business, you're not going to make it. I'm not saying that you need to stand on stage, write a book (although you may jump at the chance!) but it is about standing out in your own authentic way, with the right approach to make it work for you. This book will give you the strategies to do so. If you are fearful or stand in your darkness, let me help you to stand in the light so that you can acknowledge what you are great at doing, and share your brilliance with your clients.

The system I am sharing with you is a process that you can follow when you set up a business, starting with your idea and transforming it into a great enterprise. If you have been running a business for a while, you can review each step. Acknowledge what works well and take action on the things that you know need to be different.

There are plenty of people out there who offer part of the system, but I believe that to make a business work, you need to take each of the steps, in the right order. If you just leave one part to chance, you'll later find that something doesn't work; you'll struggle with your motivation and focus, or you won't get the results you desire.

About the book and the SUCCESS system

I have been talking about the system for a while, so let me give you more detail. The 7 step SUCCESS system that I have developed applies to business owners who are providing a one-to-one service to their clients. In this book, I'll probably lapse into talking about coaches, and when I refer to this word, please take it as 'people helpers' and will equally apply if you run any service-based business as a consultant, therapist, marketeer and more, and probably some product-based businesses. The reason it applies to this type of solopreneur is that it can be easier when you are selling a product. You can show your customer a widget and demonstrate how it works, but when you are selling a service, it can be more difficult to differentiate yourself and stand out. This intangible element makes it harder to quantify what you do and the results you give to others.

My aim in this book is two-fold. Firstly, I want to share with you the 7 step SUCCESS system that works for business owners who are providing a service to their clients. Secondly, I want to share specific ways in which you can be an expert, stand out from the crowd, and discover how to shine.

In this book, you will learn each part of the system, practise exercises to get your business on track, develop ideas and insights, and take the steps you need to achieve your own version of success.

Here are the 7 steps:

Step 1 – **S**hape your vision
Step 2 – **U**nderstand your strategy
Step 3 – **C**ultivate your confidence
Step 4 – **C**ut the crap
Step 5 – **E**xplore your expertise
Step 6 – **S**culpt your marketing plan
Step 7 – **S**et off, stand out and shine

Let me go into more detail about each step.

Shape your vision – this is a part that is often missing from businesses and one that is essential. You have to know your vision and what you want to achieve in your business to make it a success. If you don't know what you want, how will you know when you've achieved it? This is more than having a plan and is a way to develop your huge, hairy and audacious dreams, your big 'why', your passion for what you do, and the reason why you actually do it.

Understand your strategy – it's great to have your vision and your big dreams, but they will stay dreams unless you know how to make them happen. In this step, you will become clear on how you can do this, get into the detail of what needs to happen and break your ideas into bite-sized and manageable pieces. You also have to do what you might call the boring stuff – put your business plan into place, get focused on your financials, and bring your business ideas to life.

Cultivate your confidence – you might be wondering when we get into the juicy stuff about how to run a business, but I believe that the confidence part is hugely under-rated until you are in the thick of it. If you think about it, many of you reading this book have come from a corporate background and running a business is very different. This part focuses on your mindset, your confidence to do something different, your motivation to make your plans happen, and the strategies you can follow when you're struggling to get results.

Cut the crap – every day I see business owners sabotage their success. They get in their own way and let the influence of others stop them in their tracks. That is why this step is so important, to allow you to cut the crap, get out of your own way, and take every possible step to bring your plans alive. You can have all the business knowledge in the world but, unless you have the conviction to make it happen, it won't.

Explore your expertise – I'm sure that you've heard that to be successful, you need to niche or specialise, but not everyone who 'niches' does this successfully. Exploring your expertise is more than having a niche – it is about aligning your skills and knowledge to your business, doing what you love to do and funnily enough, learning how to make a financially successful business from it.

Sculpt your marketing plan – once you understand what you want to be recognised for, it makes sense to develop a plan. There are plenty of options when it comes to marketing your business, so it is important to find the ones that works for you and your clients. You will also work out how to develop your clear message, share it with the right audience and discover how you can easily attract clients. Oh, and make sales too!

Set off, stand out and shine – this final step is about learning how to leverage everything that you have learnt. You will find out how you can be the best in your area of expertise and what you can do to stand out. You will also learn simple sub-steps you can follow to write a book, stand on stage, win awards, and more, so that you become known and achieve even greater success. In this book, I'll be showing you **how** you can do this.

Just as I find with my clients, you may need more help with some areas than others, so I'll leave you to use your discretion as to how you take each step. In addition, if you need some help along your journey, just let me know and we can talk about how I can make it easy for you.

This system will apply to you whether you are a newly-qualified hypnotherapist just starting out in business, a niched career coach who wants to step up and become better known, to an experienced virtual assistant who wants to stand out from everyone else. Just spend time on the areas that work for you and then take action.

So, let me take you by the hand, lead you through the 7 steps and I'll leave you to decide what you need to do first to stand out in your business.

On the website www.HowToStandOut.co.uk you can:

- Download the exercises and activities in this book to complete at your convenience
- Get access to freebies, inspiration and even more information
- Connect with me and a community of stars who are ready to take the next step, stand out and shine in their business

Chapter 2
Step 1: Shape your vision

'Your vision will become clear only when you can look into your own heart. Who looks outside, dreams; who looks inside, awakes.' – Carl Jung

When you look at the system I outlined in my introduction, you may be thinking this: 'You don't even touch the real meaty business growth stuff until step 5, so why can't I start there?'

The first mistake made by many business owners is to *not* start at the beginning. They will jump in with their ideas, not knowing whether they will work or, they will do the most important steps later. This can result in many things – for some it will be failure, for some it will be chaos, and for some it will be a feeling that things aren't quite going to plan.

In saying that, with each of these steps, you may need to spend more time on some areas than others, but in learning the strategies, you are in effect, digging the foundations for your successful business. Once you have the foundations in place, it makes it easier to build your business, to be aligned with what you are doing, and know that every step takes you in the right direction.

Like any good plan, I believe a great place to start is having a vision and, in this case, it is about having a vision for your business. It does not have to be set in stone; it can be movable, adaptable, and changeable.

Having a clear idea of where you want to go is a great place to start and is step 1 in the SUCCESS System.

What is a vision?

Before you start to create your vision, let's begin by looking at what it means. This is the dictionary definition of vision:

- The act or power of sensing with the eyes; sight
- The act or power of anticipating that which will or may come to be
- An experience in which a thing, or event appears vividly or credibly to the mind
- A vivid, imaginative conception or anticipation

A vision is about having a clear picture of the future – your goals, your aims, your aspirations. Taking into account the dictionary definition, it is about seeing what you want to create, being excited about what you want to manifest, and making your vision powerful and compelling.

To be powerful and compelling though, your vision cannot be mediocre; it has to be amazing! It has to be one that will get you up and going even when you don't feel like it, as the pull towards achieving it will be bigger than you alone.

Why do you need a vision?

One of the messages that I shared in *The Secrets of Successful Coaches* is to start with the end in mind. When you have a vision, you are able to do this.

If you think about it, most of the successful enterprises across the world have a vision for their businesses, so it makes sense that you have one. It is said that the average person spends more time planning their holiday than their life, so if you apply the same philosophy to your business, guess what will happen?

You may be thinking that you really don't know where you want your business to be in one, two or five years' time, so how can you create a vision?

Firstly, your vision is the starting point to let your imagination run wild. We also create our visions in different ways. For some, you will find that you are logical, a left brained person, so having a list of things you want to have, or answering questions may be a good place to start. If you are a right brained, creative person, creating a vision board or mind mapping with coloured pens will help you to create your vision. Just as a taster, take time now to think about the following questions:

- What do you really want to create in your business?
- How does this fit in with your life?
- What do you want to do, be or have?
- What are the dreams for your life and business?
- Where and when do you want these dreams and goals to happen?
- Why is this important?

Secondly, in creating your vision, you are less likely to think small as you'll start thinking of all the possibilities. If you don't restrict yourself with boundaries, and the things that may hold you back, you'll think of the bigger picture and what you can really create in your life and business. It's probably wise to say at this point that you should consider both *your life* and *your business* within your vision, because when you are a solopreneur there is an overlap. As much as you may attempt to keep the two separate, when you shape your vision, the business will very much be part of your life, who you are and what you love to do – and, honestly, it won't feel like work!

Before I give you a couple of strategies to try out, here are the benefits of taking this very first step:

- You can capture your ideas
- You can think big and without boundaries or judging whether you can or can't do something
- You can take steps every day to make things happen and know what it is that you want to achieve
- You can avoid overwhelm as you can work out how to achieve each thing you want by breaking tasks into manageable chunks
- You can make effective decisions; whether activities and work that you are offered fit into that vision, and then accept or decline them
- You can start to attract the things that you want to have into your business and your life

Your 'big why'

Before you start to shape your vision, I'd like to share some concepts that will enable you to develop it further, so you have all the information you need before you make a start. One concept that I often share with my clients is around having your 'big why'.

Your 'big why' is:

- The motivation for starting your business in the first place
- The bigger reason why you show up to help others
- The bigger reason that keeps you going through the tough and difficult times
- A reason bigger than yourself

- Something that lights the fire in your belly
- What you are on this planet to do
- What you may find is your legacy

Having a 'big why' for your business is what propels you, motivates you and keeps you on top when the going gets tough. It is what gets you out of bed in the morning and enables you to achieve your vision. It is the thing that makes you step out of your comfort zone and do the things that scare you. You will find that the ultimate result of doing this thing and getting results will enable you to fulfil your 'big why' in your life and business.

You may have big goals for your business, but what is the real reason for doing what you are doing? How can you make a mark on the world, do something different and really make a difference to others?

My 'big why' is to help more coaches and solopreneurs to reach more people than I can do alone, thus enabling them to live more fulfilling and enjoyable lives. This reason motivates me to inspire others and do things like jumping out of a plane for charity, trekking to Machu Picchu, putting on big events, writing books, walking on hot coals and doing things that scare me!

Your passion and purpose

You may be thinking how your 'big why' links to your purpose, or indeed your passion?

Let's start with the word passion. When you are passionate about what you do, you do what you love to do and if you didn't need to make money, you'd be tempted to do it for free. It is something that is compelling and pulls you towards it, giving you energy, momentum, and motivation.

In contrast, your purpose is about knowing what you want and doing it because it expresses who you really are, living life 'on purpose' and living the life you are born to live. It is about living your values and it is the intention for your business and the type of people you love to work with.

With both of these, there is a very close link to your 'big why', but the difference to me is that your 'big why' is greater than your purpose. It enables you to 'get out of your own way' to do the things that you love to do.

What it boils down to is knowing what you want to do, why you want to do it, and the bigger reason behind all of this!

Thinking big

In this chapter, my aim is to help you to think big about your vision, your passion, your purpose, and your why. You could have a vision that you would like to create, but if your vision is small, will that really serve you? I assume that as you are making the time to read this business book, you are thinking big and you want to learn how to stretch yourself.

Over the last few months, there have been a couple of picture messages going viral on Facebook. One that I love shows the comfort zone in a circle, and there is an arrow pointing to another circle that says, 'This is where the magic happens.'

There is another picture that shows the comfort zone in a circle with words that express things that happen there, such as 'mediocre', 'tired', 'fear', 'average', 'What if I can't?' Then outside the comfort zone circle, there are words such as 'fearless', 'excitement', 'wealth', 'belief', 'passion', 'confidence', 'dreams', 'financial freedom' and more. I am sure you get the picture.

There are three elements to a comfort zone – the comfort zone, the stretch zone, and the panic zone.

The first, your comfort zone, is where, as you can see above, you feel comfortable, perhaps in a rut and are not doing anything to grow. It is where you feel safe, and it is average, boring, and a little mediocre.

When you stretch yourself and do something new or different, you will be entering the stretch zone. This is where you go when you take calculated risks, or you do something new that perhaps scares you a little. You will be stretching yourself but in doing so, you will be embracing new experiences. You will be saying, 'What if I can?', rather than 'What if I can't?' and you will be excited, fearless and following your dreams. You may not be completely fearless, of course, but you will be stretching what originally felt comfortable.

Lastly, you have your panic zone. It makes you worried and fearful, and is not a place I recommend you visit very often.

Most people in life spend a lot of their time in their comfort zone. Probably around 80% of the population spend 80% of their time there! Do you want to be one of these? The trick is to start to spend more time in your stretch zone. In doing this, you will ultimately stretch your comfort zone, so that what used to scare you a little becomes the norm, and you do more things that stretch you.

When you think about your vision, what will it take for you to think big and outside of your comfort zone? To be honest, I wonder whether it is really worth creating a vision unless you are willing to think big. If you restrict yourself, you'll be staying small, whereas I can't wait to give you the space and the strategies for you to see the possibilities of what you can really create.

I want to share a few last comments about thinking big. Some of you may struggle to do this if you just cannot see the bigger vision, or perhaps you categorise yourself as a person who cannot visualise the future.

I urge you to try the exercises in this book and prove yourself wrong.

In addition, you may be worried that in thinking big you will become overwhelmed and unable to take steps towards achieving your bigger goals. You may think that this will paralyse you or stop you dreaming in the first place. Do not let that impede you. In step 2, we'll look at how you can break your vision into manageable chunks so you can work towards achieving what you want every day.

The Fisherman's story

I would like to share with you a story. The origin of this story is unknown although it illustrates an important point:

One day, a fisherman was lying on a beautiful beach, with his fishing pole propped up in the sand and his solitary line cast out into the sparkling blue surf. He was enjoying the warmth of the afternoon sun and the prospect of catching a fish.

About that time, a businessman came walking down the beach, trying to relieve some of the stress of his work day. He noticed the fisherman sitting on the beach and decided to find out why this fisherman was fishing instead of working harder to make a living for himself and his family. 'You aren't going to catch many fish that way,' said the businessman to the fisherman. 'You should be working rather than lying on the beach!'

The fisherman looked up at the businessman, smiled and replied, 'And what will my reward be?' 'Well, you can get bigger nets and catch more fish!' was the businessman's answer. 'And then what will my reward be?' asked the fisherman, still smiling. The businessman replied, 'You will make money and you'll be able to buy a boat, which will then result in larger catches of fish!' 'And then what will my reward be?' asked the fisherman again. The businessman was beginning to get a little irritated with the fisherman's questions. 'You can buy a bigger boat, and hire some people to work for you!' he said.

'And then what will my reward be?' repeated the fisherman. The businessman was getting angry. 'Don't you understand? You can build up a fleet of fishing boats, sail all over the world, and let all your employees catch fish for you!' Once again the fisherman asked, 'And then what will my reward be?' The businessman was red with rage and shouted at the fisherman, 'Don't you understand that you can become so rich that you will never have to work for your living again! You can spend all the rest of your days sitting on this beach, looking at the sunset. You won't have a care in the world!'

The fisherman, still smiling, looked up and said, 'And what do you think I'm doing right now?'

Are you the fisherman or are you the businessman? You can interpret this story in different ways. It may be that you don't need huge riches to be happy, or, it may help you to realise how you want to feel when you get what you want. When you create your vision, consider what success means to you.

- Is it about power, wealth, a feeling or something else?
- Is it measurable?
- What do you really want to have in your life and why?
- Is it about you and your family or is it about giving back or a combination of the two?
- Is it always about the future or is it also about the 'Now'?

Do not wait to live the life you want to live now, even if your vision changes as your life moves forward.

How is your mindset?

Lastly, before I share with you three great strategies to shape your vision, I want to ask you about your mindset. One of the biggest moments in my business was when I realigned my own mindset. When I qualified as a coach, I labelled myself as a coach; I introduced myself as a coach, and saw myself as a coach. I focused my mindset on my profession. It took me a while to focus on my clients, the solution I provided for them, and ultimately the fact that I was actually running a business. It was a profound moment for me when I realised that I was a business owner with coaching as one of the tools in my toolkit. I am a NLP Master Practitioner, I have fifteen years of training experience, I am a Human Resources professional, Coach, Mentor, DISC and Emotional Intelligence Practitioner, Firewalk Instructor, speaker, author, and so much more. This shift in mindset made a huge difference to me and my business.

In looking at your mindset, this will impact on your vision as you will start to see where you want to go, how you can grow and then achieve the successes that you desire.

How to create your vision

In this book, I will share with you 3 different ways to develop your vision. Remember you can also go to www.HowToStandOut.co.uk to download any of these resources including a vision hypnosis recording that will help you to bring your vision alive.

Your ideal day

This is a great visualisation that I came across when I saw Jairek Robbins (the son of the top American Life Coach, Anthony Robbins) at an event in 2011, and this is my interpretation of the exercise. I suggest you record this text in your own voice and sit down and listen to it just like a normal visualisation or, alternatively, sit down and contemplate your ideal life whilst listening to relaxing or inspiring music.

Visualise your ideal day

Imagine waking up on the morning of your absolute wonderful, most ideal day ...

Where are you living? What do you see when you first wake up? What is the first thing you think about? How do you spend your morning?

Take yourself through the morning and on to lunchtime. What is your health and energy like? What do you eat? What are you doing?

Consider your relationships – who are you with? Who would you like to be with?

Think about your emotional state – how do you feel and what do you like about this feeling?

Reflect on your business, your job or your career – what is happening here on your most wonderful day? What is different and how is it manifesting itself?

And your finances – what is the situation on your most ideal and wonderful day?

Take yourself through your ideal afternoon on your most wonderful day? What are you excited about?

Move yourself through to the evening – what have you done, achieved, accomplished, reached or realised on your most wonderful and ideal day? What are you planning, or intending to do to continue to have ideal and most wonderful days in the future?

When you are ready, open your eyes. How do you feel? What insights did you have? Make sure you write these down.

Creating a vision board

Another way to create your vision is by developing a vision board for your life, your business, or anything else that is important to you.

A vision or mood board helps you to visually create a picture of what you want your life to be like. Often used in conjunction with the Law of Attraction, it can help you to magnetise what you want into your life.

How to create a vision board

1. Start to create your vision and goals for the coming year. What do you want to do, be or have this year? What are your goals, dreams or ideals?
2. Prepare to create your vision board. I like to take an A3 piece of card, a selection of my favourite magazines, glue, and scissors. Then sit down somewhere where you have some time and space. Put on an uplifting piece of music too!
3. Taking your goals for the coming year, go through the magazines and cut out any pictures, words or phrases that resonate with you and your goals. Or you could print off some of your favourite quotes from your computer

and use different materials and textures if you are feeling creative.
4. Once you have cut out your pictures, words, etc., arrange and stick them onto your board.
5. Place your board where you can see it every day to remind you of your goals.
6. Take action!

Your purpose statement

You may have sat down from time to time and thought about your passion, your life's purpose and how you can do what you love in your business, but it is not always easy to put it into practice.

If you have thought about your purpose and passion, are these thoughts all yours? Ideas of success come from all sorts of areas: your parents, the media, society, your peers and friends, and the agreed norm. What is *your* real purpose and passion?

What is your goal for your business – your big goal? Perhaps this is around client numbers, a financial goal, or something else? Write down your current goal right now, right here.

My goal:

Why do you want this goal?

What then?

What will you have?

Repeat these questions until you don't get any more answers.

You will probably find that you are left with a goal based on your purpose and passion. If you could summarise this into a purpose statement in one sentence that you can see and affirm every day, what would this statement be?

What single step can you take each day to manifest this in your life?

How can you make sure that you look at this before you plan each day or take each step?

How will this stop you succumbing to procrastination and fear?

Is there anything else you need to do to adjust it to make it even more powerful?

What 5 things can you do in your business right now to move yourself closer to your big dream?

1.

2.

3.

4.

5.

What might stop you?

I do hope that these 3 techniques help you to create your vision, but there are a few vital things to consider before we move onto the next step.

Avoiding overwhelm

It can be particularly overwhelming at the start of your business journey. As I mentioned earlier, not only do you have to be great at your profession, you also have to learn how to run a business. On top of that, if you've been in the corporate world all of your life, it can be a shock to the system. It is easy to not know where to start and in feeling this way, you don't start. This then leads to frustration and to be honest, a very vicious circle.

Having a vision is great as it gives you a route map, whether it is in writing or in pictures, so the very first step is to look at your journey. The steps in this book will give you a solid structure, so it may well be worth reading on before stopping to plan. In the meantime, let me give you some tips.

Overwhelm occurs when you have no direction and, you feel quite literally 'buried under a deep mass' or 'defeated'. One of the worst things about overwhelm is that it can stop you achieving anything and leave you paralysed and ineffective. Therefore, I'd like to give you some strategies to get on top of what needs to be done, so you can get on with building your business.

Goal setting

I'm sure you've come across goals, objectives and plans, and setting SMART goals (especially if you are a coach!) If not, SMART stands for Specific, Measurable, Achievable, Realistic/Relevant and Time-bound, and goals must be aligned to these principles. It is always great to be reminded of your goals and goal setting from time to time to keep you on the right track. Like setting personal goals, setting business goals provides you with direction and motivation. It is essential to set the right goals – ones that will keep your business on track, rather than derail it.

Setting goals, aims or objectives before taking action helps you to:

- Have a target to aim towards which means that all your actions are targeted towards that aim rather than getting distracted or losing focus
- Develop a good sense of direction
- Feel motivated, especially when you start to achieve your objectives
- Evaluate how you are doing against your target

You can see why it is important to set goals, but, as I

have just mentioned, it is equally important to set the right goals – having a vision will give you the long-term plan, but what has to happen first for you to achieve it? Breaking it down into bite-sized chunks with smaller target dates is one suggestion.

Prioritisation

It is all well and good having goals, but unless you prioritise, you might not get the right things achieved in the right order. It is easy to do the things that you enjoy doing rather than the things that will give you the best results.

If you struggle to prioritise, then write yourself a list of what you need to achieve and then give each item an A, B or C rating. The A items are the urgent ones, probably the ones that need to be done right away. The B items are the ones that are important, but may not be so urgent. With the C items, do you need to do these, delegate them or ditch them altogether? I am most effective when I write myself a list at the end of each day for the next. It stops me from dwelling on what I might need to do and gives me focus when I go into the office the next morning.

Avoiding procrastination

The A, B, C technique above was adapted from a tip in Brian Tracy's book, *Eat That Frog*, and this very phrase is the one I want to use here. To achieve your vision, you do need to eat your frog and do the thing that you don't want to do. Perhaps it is the call you don't want to make, or the report you don't want to write. Then, when you don't do it, it becomes bigger, and more difficult to manage as you start to worry (or the frog becomes bigger and uglier). The trick is to make sure that you eat your frog first thing each day. I'm sure you will find that actually eating your frog isn't as bad as you think it is. Not only that, if you do it straight away, you won't be wasting your time and energy worrying, contemplating, or thinking 'What if?'

Moving onto step 2

Before we move onto step 2, let's take a moment to reflect on the first step in the SUCCESS System.

By now I am sure you will see why having a clear vision and your 'big why' are important parts of your business. If you are a big picture person, you'll be able to see the future in technicolour, but will you do anything to make it happen? Unless you know how to break it down into manageable chunks, it will appear huge and overwhelming. This leads us to step 2 – understanding your strategy to make your big dreams happen!

Chapter 3
Step 2: Understand your strategy

'You don't learn to walk by following rules. You learn by doing, and by falling over.' – Richard Branson

Now is the time to put into place the structure in your business to make it work for you. Step 2 is about understanding your business strategy. This comprises your business structure, the legal frameworks, and the initial steps you need to take. You may want to jump into some of the later steps in the system, as they may seem more fun or easier to do but, when you have your business strategies in place, they will keep you on the right track to ultimately reaching your vision.

Your business structure

The very first thing you need to think about is your business structure. Don't concern yourself too much as it is something that can change as your business grows and develops, but an important consideration all the same.

What do I mean by business structure? I am talking about whether you want to trade as a sole trader, limited company or partnership. For many small businesses where there is one owner, being a sole trader is the best option, so let me explain the key differences (as applicable in the UK).

Sole trader – this is the simplest solution when you set up your business as a solopreneur, although you are responsible for any debts of the business. On the plus side, you don't have to produce a balance sheet or have your accounts audited, but on the negative side, it may not seem so professional to potential clients, especially to corporations.

Partnership – if you are working in partnership with another person, you may wish to consider this option as you will need to set out a formal legal agreement documenting the arrangement.

Limited company – this is more complex than the other options as you will become a director of the company and your liability is limited. However, you are bound by the Companies Act legislation and have legal duties to prepare audited accounts and filing these with Companies House. This is the best option if you have big plans and want to work with corporations.

Deciding your trading status is just the start. Whichever option you choose at this stage, one of the first things that you need to do is tell the Inland Revenue that you are trading, so that they can issue you with a tax return to complete. In addition, you will need to pay National Insurance contributions. This applies even if you are still in full or part-time employment. However, it is earnings dependent, so if you are earning less than the threshold, you can apply for the payments to cease as you grow your business. In time, you will also need to consider VAT if your turnover is £77,000 or above per year (in 2012).

For more information, check out: www.companieshouse.gov.uk and www.hmrc.gov.uk. Other considerations you may wish to research are employing others, if this is appropriate, although many solopreneurs work on a project-by-project basis with other solopreneurs, where an employment relationship does not take place.

In addition, you may also want to look at franchising and licensing, depending on the type of business you are running.

Your business plan

A business plan is a formal statement of your business goals, the reasons why you want to attain these goals, and the plan for reaching them. It may also contain background information about the organisation and the team attempting to reach those goals.

A written plan for your business is essential if you are seeking finance. You will have to prove to a lender that you have a realistic plan for your business. One of the best things about being a solopreneur is that you are unlikely to need start-up capital if you are working for yourself, by yourself, and providing a service to your clients. Many great businesses have been set up with minimal costs in a spare room. Setting up a business doesn't have to be expensive, but even with this in mind, having a plan is important.

Business planning is essential for any business, or at least if you want it to be a success. It does not have to be a full twenty-page business plan and could consist of some words and ideas on the back of an envelope, but make sure you plan all the same.

If you start with the end in mind, it means that every step you take in your business is in the right direction rather than wasting time with ad hoc or unproductive activities that don't enable you to reach your end goals.

If you have a vision and have undertaken one or more of the exercises in step 1, you can ask yourself, when you make a decision in your business, whether it takes you towards or away from your goal.

Your plan may include a number of areas, some of which I will cover later in the book, so this is a good time to tell you that the most important part of a business plan is that it is not a static document. It will change, adapt, and be modified as your business does the same.

What to include in a business plan

1. Summary of your business:
a. Business name
b. Business idea
c. Key success factors
d. Location of the business

2. Team:
a. You (and your team if applicable)
b. Your skills, capabilities
c. Support networks

3. Service:
a. Description of your service
b. Target market
c. Niche/specialism
d. Unique selling proposition
e. SWOT analysis
f. Ideal client profile

4. Sales and marketing:
a. Pricing structure and packages
b. Marketing plan
c. Promotional plans

5. Resources:
a. Suppliers
b. Equipment
c. Legislative requirements

6. Business expenditure, costs and projected profits:
   a. What you project to spend during the first couple of years
   b. Your budget for activities, such as marketing, training, mentoring
   c. Your projected monthly/yearly income

I am sure you'll be looking at this list and be thinking 'Where do I start?' but, as I mentioned, it doesn't have to be complex. I will talk you through some of these areas in later chapters. Simply, you need to just get on and define your business and plan for your future. It is up to you how much detail you want to include in your plan but, if you start with the end in mind, it will be easier for you later.

SWOT Analysis

It is about time that you put this book down and did a short exercise to get your mind moving and make your business feel like a reality. Doing a SWOT analysis is an extremely useful tool for understanding and decision-making for all sorts of situations. SWOT is an acronym for Strengths, Weaknesses, Opportunities, and Threats.

Completing a SWOT

Start by considering your business goal (this is also a great exercise to assess your own personal SWOT). Consider each of the sections separately and write your ideas in a notebook or below:

Strengths:

Weaknesses:

Opportunities:

Threats:

If you are struggling to come up with ideas, let me give you some questions to consider under each section.

Strengths

What skills and capabilities do you have?
In what areas do you excel?
What qualifications, accreditations or experience make you unique?
What would other people consider to be your strengths?
What qualities, values or beliefs make you stand out from others?

Weaknesses

What are the gaps in your capabilities and what skills do you need to develop?
In which areas could you improve?
What would other people consider to be your weaknesses?
What personal difficulties do you need to overcome to reach your goal?

Opportunities

What opportunities are available to you?
What external influences can help you to achieve success?
Who do you know who can support you to help you achieve your goal?

Threats

What obstacles are you facing?
What external influences may hinder your success?
Who or what could get in the way of you achieving your goal?

When carrying out a SWOT analysis on your business, you may also choose to go deeper into economic influences, your competition, information and research, trends and new technologies and ideas that may impact your business. If you have an awareness of each of these areas, it will help you to start to shape your business.

Your branding and logo

Branding is at the core of your business and is based on your values, attributes, your strengths, and your goals, and how you communicate these to your clients. Your brand is what creates your reputation in the marketplace and can influence your business's ability to stand out from everyone else in your industry.

At this stage you may be unsure of the brand of your business, and you may be a little hazy on your values (which was covered in one of the chapters of *The Secrets of Successful Coaches)*, but you need to start somewhere. At the very least, by now you should have a vision for your business.

When people think of branding, many think of a logo and business name, and as much as these are important, they are not the only consideration when branding your business. Although I do remember one of my clients telling me once that when she had her business name and logo, it made her business seem real.

When you think about your branding, think about how you want people to perceive you, what you do, how you do it, and the message you want to share. You may choose to work with a branding expert, whether it is full branding for your business, or a business name and logo that you create together. There is nothing worse than seeing another company with the same logo or name, or a brand that does not appear professional.

When it comes to naming your business, this is an area where many people struggle, so let me give you a few tips.

When I set up my business, I went through many deliberations over my business name. When I did my coaching training, we were told to use our own names, but unless your name is unique, it doesn't make this easy. The alternative option is to choose a business name that is inspiring, means something to you or is something to which your clients and prospects can relate.

I suggest that you choose a name that will stand the test of time as your business develops. You may change your area of expertise, your niche, you may tweak the type of work you do, the problems you solve and the clients that you work with.

Your business name is just one part of your branding, so make sure it is consistent with who you are and what you do. Think about the image it portrays and how you feel when introducing yourself using this name. It may mean something to you, but will it mean anything to others?

When you research your business name, make sure the website domain of your preferred brand is available – both the .co.uk and the .com too – then register them for your business. This will save confusion in the future if another business chooses the same name. If your business name can be spelt in many different ways, register the various combinations as well. For example, a name with two or more words could be spelt with hyphens between each word or without.

When you check your domain names, make sure that the words, when they have been typed without spaces, don't spell something that may be difficult to remember, rude, or something that will be frequently misspelt.

Lastly, check Companies House for your preferred name. Although you may decide to be a sole trader rather than limited company, it makes sense to check whether your name is already registered to another company.

The legal stuff

I've already touched on some of the things you need to do when you set up in business. You need to make sure that you are registered as self-employed and, depending upon your business type, there are other things to consider too.

Data protection – if you store or keep information on others, you will need to register with the Information Commissioner. At the time of writing, if you are a small company in the UK, you will be paying £35 per year. In paying your fee, you confirm that you are complying with the Data Protection Act 1998, and there are 8 principles that you need to follow.

The main considerations are that you fairly and lawfully process and keep information, that the information is kept secure, such as in a locked filing cabinet and that computerised information is password protected, and that you don't share information without the person's permission. This includes client information, contact details, emails, your newsletter list, etc. Go to www.ico.gov.uk or www.dataprotectionact.org for more information.

Insurance – for many professions, insurance is required to cover malpractice, professional liability and public liability. Like any insurance, you hope that you will never need it, yet it is better to have the insurance in place to cover you and your business.

When you are considering insurance, go to your training company for advice in the first instance, as some will be affiliated with an insurance company and may provide discounts for their trainees. Some insurance policies will also cover you for a range of complementary therapies if you are trained in these areas.

Other things you need to know

I know that you want to get going but, before we move to the next stage, there are other things to consider.

Membership – you may decide to become a member of a body affiliated to your profession. For example, in the coaching profession, there are various bodies to which you can choose to belong and which give you various benefits. These may include (but are not limited to) credibility, up-to-date information on latest industry developments, a regular magazine and support through meetings, ongoing training, development opportunities and more.

Managing the financials – I mentioned earlier that you need to register with the Inland Revenue, and one of the business basics is to manage your financials. You also may consider getting a bookkeeper or an accountant, or use a bookkeeping software system to manage your finances (I use Kashflow). Whatever you decide, keep on top of your income and outgoings, and keep money aside for tax and other expenses. Whilst talking about financials, consider how you wish to take payment, set up a separate bank account and you may consider using PayPal, a credit card system or something similar.

Premises – you may well decide to work from home for now and, if you do so, consider checking your insurance if you are inviting clients into your home. There are also offices and meeting rooms that you can rent by the hour, half-day, day or for longer periods of time. You may also meet clients in hotels or cafés if it is appropriate. Working for yourself can be a lonely business, so having various options as to where you can work are important areas to consider.

Telephone – you may choose to use your mobile, get a business line, or use your home phone number.

Check out www.vonage.com for a VOIP (Internet line) and www.skype.com. If you are talking to clients on the phone, you will also need to consider other equipment, such as a computer, headset, and organising the best working environment that suits you.

Getting your business off the ground

All of this preparation is important, but what about getting your business off the ground? Where do you go next?

Create your website

It is important to have a website in this day and age, but it doesn't have to cost a fortune. Having a simple site is a great starting point as it gives you a web presence and you can add your content as you go, but remember again to start with the end in mind!

If you are not tech-savvy, setting up your website may feel overwhelming, so find someone to do it for you. This is the sort of advice that I'll be sharing throughout this book – don't forget it is your job to stand out from the crowd and do what you do well, so do the same for your website and give it to someone who is an expert.

There are many platforms you can consider. I prefer Wordpress (www.wordpress.org), as a good web designer will be able to set up the template for you and you will be able to easily update and add pages. This will be more cost-effective than asking your web designer to make tweaks for you. I guarantee that there will be plenty of changes, especially in the early days. In addition, Wordpress gives you an integrated blog that enables you to share regular, new content. As Google and other search engines love new content, this will help you with your search engine rankings.

I'll be talking more about websites when I get to Chapter 7, and will be sharing my tips to create a community via your website that enables you to build your business quickly and easily.

Business cards

In this section, I have mentioned some of the technological aspects that you need to get your head around and touched on branding. But you won't get business if you don't venture away from your computer. Networking is likely to be part of your strategy and, traditionally, when you network you will have business cards. I would like to challenge this thought. I believe the most important thing to do is to collect other people's cards and information, and follow up with them, but if you choose to get your own business cards, I think it only right that I share my advice.

Business card tips

1. Get your business cards professionally designed and printed, or at the very least choose high quality card (around 400gsm in thickness). Include your unique business logo and your contact details. Ultimately, your business cards reflect your brand, so make sure you are proud of them. Remember that your business cards have two sides for a reason, so use them!

2. Be different – include a photograph of you (as long as it is a good professional picture!) This will enable people to remember you, put a face to your name and, as a solopreneur, **you** are your business.

3. Tell people about the results you provide

rather than your profession. People don't want to know that you are a coach, therapist or something else, they want to know about what you do, the results you provide, and the people you work with.

4. Include your social media contact details. The most successful solopreneurs are on Facebook, LinkedIn, Twitter, YouTube and more. Make sure you include these details so that the recipient can connect with you online (I'll be touching on that later).

5. Check your details. I know that this may seem obvious, but it never fails to surprise me how many business cards have numbers crossed out, email addresses changed or other amendments made. So before you go to print, check, double and triple check! Make sure you have all the details that someone may need such as your website, phone number, email address, etc.

6. Keep it simple and clear. You don't want to crowd your business cards with all your details, but it happens all the time. If you have separate businesses, you may choose to have two different cards so that people don't get confused by what you do.

7. Include a call to action. Many business cards just end up filed in a drawer or at the very best in a business card folder, so what can you do to be different? Include a call to action so that the recipient does something, such as signs up for your free report (more on that later), books a free taster session with you, or follows you on Twitter.

If you're not sure what to include on your cards, study the business cards of other people in your industry. What do you like and don't like and why? Who would you like to model? What can you do differently to stand out?

Know your numbers

One last tip in this chapter before we move on. It is essential to know your numbers. To be successful in business, you need to know your cash flow, your income and outgoings, how much it costs to attract and retain a customer, where your clients are coming from, how many people are on your mailing list, and so much more. So don't leave it to chance – know your numbers, review them regularly, and you'll be on the path to even more success.

Moving onto step 3

Before we move onto step 3, take a moment to reflect on the first couple of steps in the SUCCESS System.

By now, you will have a clear vision and you will have worked out how to make this a reality. You will have also started to put the structure in place to take the next steps. Although you may be ready to jump right in, let me make you aware of what might stop you and some of the barriers you could face.

Chapter 4
Step 3: Cultivate your confidence

'Believe in yourself! Have faith in your abilities! Without a humble but reasonable confidence in your own powers you cannot be successful or happy.'
– Norman Vincent Peale

I believe that one of the keys to success in business is having confidence. Actually, it is more than just confidence – it is about having a success mindset. You can have all the business and marketing knowledge in the world but, unless you have the ability to develop the confidence to make it happen, you are going to struggle to make your business a success.

In the book *Confidence Booster Workout* by Martin Perry, this is how he describes confidence:

'Being confident means feeling positive about what you can do, and not worrying about what you can't do, but having the will to learn. Self-confidence is the oil that smoothly turns the wheels of the relationship between you, your capability – that is, your natural talents, skills and potential – and your ability to make good that capability.'

It is about being sure of your own skills and having a positive outlook on life, and, being willing to develop these abilities. There are many advantages to cultivating your confidence. You will feel more positive about your goals, you will be more resilient when you face challenges, and you are going to be able to recognise and celebrate your successes. One of the ways in which you can achieve greater confidence in business is to be aware of your mindset and, if necessary, develop and grow your mindset.

The word mindset means:

- A set of beliefs or a way of thinking that determines one's behaviour, outlook and mental attitude
- A set of assumptions, methods or notions held by a person
- How someone approaches a situation – their attitudes and ideas

This chapter is focusing on developing your confidence, watching out for what stops you, giving you strategies to be more certain, and developing the ability to go for what you want to achieve. If I haven't convinced you already, when you have a success mindset, you will:

- Be focused on success – whatever this means to you
- Be willing to change your assumptions, beliefs and ideas
- Have an approach that is focused on abundance rather than lack
- Be willing to take risks and step out of your comfort zone
- Feel uncertainty, although you will be taking steps to be, do or have what you want
- Have the courage to take action
- Be prepared to learn from mistakes
- Be focused on positive rather than negative intentions
- See challenges as opportunities
- Always be striving for something more
- Be finding and living your life's purpose

- Be growing and developing your confidence in business

Before I share with you strategies of how to achieve this, I would like to explain why having confidence and a success mindset is important, and what happens if you don't have the right mindset. Then I'll share with you some strategies for success.

Why you might struggle with confidence

If you have never run a business before, learning all you need to know can be a shock. Firstly, you may be doing a skill that is new to you, and secondly, you need to learn how to run a business.

I talked about your comfort zone in step 1 and this may be a great opportunity to review that section. What you will find in business is that you will be stretching your comfort zone every day. Whether you are learning a new technology, making cold or warm sales calls, networking with other entrepreneurs, or telling people that you have decided to run a business, it may be new, exciting, and ... scary.

Facing setbacks or challenges can have an impact on your confidence and cause self-doubt. You may even wonder why you set up your business in the first place. Therefore, developing strategies to cultivate your confidence is important.

Ultimately, there are two parts to confidence – what you exhibit outwardly and how you feel inwardly. You may see people who look confident; perhaps they are an extrovert and give the perception of being confident, but may not feel it inside. Then there is internal confidence, which is a feeling of being certain, of trusting and knowing that everything will be OK.

Develop excellence in communication

This seems like a great time to tell you about an NLP tool – the Communications Model which helps you to understand how communication works. In simplest terms, it shows how individuals make sense of the world through their senses and how this impacts on the behaviour that is demonstrated as a result.

Every day we have billions of pieces of information coming into our psyche through our senses of sight, hearing, feeling (both physical touch and internal feeling), smell and taste. Much of this information is processed by our subconscious mind, as our conscious mind can only cope with about 5-9 chunks of information at any one time. Many things we do in life are automatic, for example, we don't need to consciously be aware of how to breathe, walk or talk (unless we are having problems in one of these areas which requires conscious thought) or the many other things we do each day.

So what happens next? Our subconscious mind filters this information. It will delete that which is no longer relevant, distort things so that they fit in with our view of the world, and generalise so that we can make sense of similar situations and experiences. This happens in an instant, based on our values, beliefs, experiences, memories, decisions, and experiences in our life. Once we have filtered the information we make an internal representation of the situation, whether this is positive or negative. This affects the state we are in and our physiology, and how we communicate to others through our behaviour.

Let me give you an example. If you are driving along the motorway and another vehicle cuts you up causing you to brake suddenly or swerve, you may choose to communicate in a certain way! Much of the response you give will depend on your past experiences and memories, and all of this happens in an instant, without your conscious mind playing much part:

- If you are feeling relaxed and serene you may not react at all; you will just carry on as normal to your destination
- If you have had a rushed and busy day, you may react quite differently
- If the vehicle is a white van and you are fed up with white vans, this may evoke a specific response!
- If you have had an accident in the past, this may also affect the way you react

I'm sure with these simple examples, you can see how your subconscious mind, your memories, your experiences and more, affect the way you communicate. Ultimately, these have an impact on your confidence. If your experiences in the past may not have been so positive, it is easy to transpose these thoughts and beliefs on the way you face the future.

Values and beliefs

It is worth spending a few moments looking at your values and beliefs (which, as mentioned earlier, I explained in more detail in my first book). Values are those things that are important to you, and beliefs are those things that you believe are true. Many of your values and beliefs have been developed and influenced by your family and peers, their attitudes and philosophies, all of which have impacted upon your life.

When you know your personal values it makes it easier to create a business that is truly aligned to these values. You will know what is important to you and how you can incorporate these values into your business.

Being aware of your beliefs is equally important. As Henry Ford said, 'Whether you believe you can or you can't, you are right.' As you will have seen by the definition of mindset, beliefs play an important role in terms of how you approach a situation. In my research for *The Secrets of Successful Coaches*, I discovered that having a strong self-belief is essential in business.

Let me share something which explains this in more detail.

Your beliefs affect the thoughts you have; those thoughts inform the feelings you have about the beliefs which in turn, influence your behaviour, your actions, your results and the consequences. This then affects your beliefs.

Think about it this way. If you believe that clients are never going to be able to afford to pay you, you'll be telling people why you think this way. You are unlikely to ask people to pay you, you probably won't value yourself, and then you won't be able to share your gift and grow your business. At worst, it will be a very expensive hobby!

On the other hand, if you believe that you have a solution to a client's problem and you believe in the benefits of that solution, you'll be telling everyone about this programme or system, which is more likely to get you results, and this will reinforce your beliefs.

The problem is that you have many thousands of thoughts every day and you need to decide which ones to hold onto and which ones to ditch, especially as, for many people, many of these are negative. 90% of your thoughts are the same thoughts that you had yesterday, so unless you break out of the cycle, you will struggle to achieve the successes that you desire in your business.

People and situations cannot make you feel in a

certain way. It is your reactions that make you feel this way, whether these reactions are positive or negative. These can influence your beliefs and the actions you take. Sometimes you will do things because you have always done them, when you all you need to do is to implement new habits.

If you are not feeling very confident, you may project yourself with uncertainty. If a person notices this, it will influence their response to you. For example, your uncertainty may make someone less sure of your intentions or diminish their confidence in what you have to say.

Let's say you need to make a decision. Do you choose to create a vicious circle, where you go around the same ineffective and demotivating loop time and time again? Or, do you choose to create a virtuous circle where you get amazing results and you gain more confidence and self-belief?

If you want to change your habits, make the decision to do this. It takes just twenty-one days to change a habit, so do something different to make a positive impact on your life and business.

How motivated are you?

Your motivation can also have an impact on your confidence and vice versa. One thing I have noticed is that many people give up work to start their own business simply because they are not motivated by their current employment. In fact, when they start their own business, they realise that motivation is even more important. They no longer have someone else telling them what they need to do, when they need to do it, and how.

Motivation will affect your success and, if you have created a vicious circle, your motivation is likely to be low. This is a major reason why being aware of your mindset is important in business and that you need to create a circle that is virtuous.

So, what can you do to increase your own motivation and ultimately your success in business?

There are many strategies that you can follow, but first I suggest that you understand your own motivation, as having this self-awareness will influence the degree of success you achieve.

Individuals often have a preference to either internal or external motivation. External motivation is that which comes from outside of you, which is often one of the reasons that solopreneurs struggle in business, as you will be normally be working by yourself.

External motivation takes place when you want to do a job because it will give you external feedback, for example, in terms of praise or a reaction from someone else, rather than from your own internal value system.

Internal motivation comes from inside you and causes you to do a good job or complete a task because you feel good when you have done it. When you are internally motivated, you operate from your own values and don't need praise from another person.

If you think about it, when you are working for yourself, most of your feedback comes from yourself rather than an external party, which can impact on your success, especially if you are externally motivated.

Knowing how you work and what your preferences are is important for achieving success in business. It is also useful to know whether you are motivated *towards* success. For example, you may want to achieve something because of the rewards you will receive. Recognise whether you are motivated *away* from something to avoid pain or discomfort. For example, you may do things because of fear of what won't happen if you don't take action. As an aside, the conscious mind does not process negatives, so be aware of your language too. If you 'don't want to be poor', your subconscious mind will be deleting the negative; it does not recognise the 'don't' in the sentence. So focus your mind on what you do want instead, e.g., 'I want to be financially abundant' or something more specific which focuses on your goal. Let me give you an example. If I say to you, 'Don't think of a blue elephant', what happens? Enough said!

Just think how much improving your motivation will enhance your confidence and belief in your abilities.

How can you improve your confidence and mindset?

There are various strategies that you can put into place and you will find more in the next chapter when I talk more about avoiding self sabotage. In the meantime, here are a few of my favourite tips.

Confidence and mindset tips

1. Act as if you are confident, even if deep down you are not sure that you are. When you go into a new situation, take a deep breath, put your shoulders back, smile and then just do it. Just by taking that first step is a great place to start as you are showing your subconscious that you are willing to step outside of your comfort zone and take action.

2. Believe in the actions you take and develop your confidence to make it happen. Be aware of your strengths and recognise when you need support.

3. Focus on what you want to achieve – your big

goals – and take steps each day to get there. Take the strategies from step one, learn how to prioritise, and eat your frog. Just make sure it is the right frog and don't get distracted from what you want to achieve. When you know what you want rather than what you don't want, it will make your intentions much clearer.

4. Visualise your success. Sports psychologists help successful athletes to use visualisation to enable them to create the right mental state in which to engage in their sport. Whether this is an image of winning a gold medal or breaking a personal best, the aim is to achieve a state of flow. This is an internal state that energises and aligns emotions with the task in hand. When the brain creates an image (whether real or imaginary), it gives rise to emotional states that will evoke behaviour. Changing the way you think will change the way you feel and, therefore, change the way you behave.

5. Model someone who is excellent at what you want to do. Spend time with them and learn from them. In my first book I found people who were very good at what I wanted to do (they ran successful coaching businesses) and by following their strategies, I transformed my business. Learn from their values, beliefs, language, and traits. Pick the best bits and authentically add these into your life. It is not about copying, but about being aware of what they do that enables them to stand out from the crowd.

6. Learn to celebrate your successes and how you can create more of these. Look after yourself, get motivated and keep focused. Keep a success list, a journal or something else that reminds you of how far you have come.

7. My top tip to develop your successful business is to get a coach or mentor who will encourage you, support you and inspire you to keep on track and achieve the results you want in your business.

Moving onto step 4

I would like to end this chapter by talking about *Someday Isle.* This is a concept that Brian Tracy introduced to me. He talks about this idyllic holiday resort and, like many small resorts, it has its own culture, language and beliefs. The types of things that were said on this Isle were ... 'Someday I will grow my business ...' 'Someday I will follow my dreams ...' and 'Someday I will give up my day job ...'

It may feel safe to be on *Someday Isle,* but if you are there yourself, are you really achieving what you want right now? This is the difference between those who run a mediocre business and those who are successful, as they have the mindset to achieve the success they desire.

Anthony Robbins says, 'The only reason you don't have exactly what you want is the story you keeping telling yourself about why you can't have it or don't have it already.'

This leads me to take you onto the next step of the journey which will enable you to cut the crap that stops you from travelling to a new resort and making big things happen!

Chapter 5
Step 4: Cut the crap

'Inaction breeds doubt and fear. Action breeds confidence and courage. If you want to conquer fear, do not sit home and think about it. Go out and get busy.' – Dale Carnegie

You may be wondering what the difference is between cultivating your confidence and cutting the crap. Yes, there is an overlap, but there is also a distinction.

When I suggest that you cut the crap, it is about removing the barriers to your success. It is about getting rid of the excuses, the fears, feelings of overwhelm, and managing the opinions of others, which may hinder even the most confident people.

This step of the system will be informing you about how you might sabotage your success. We will discover what gets in the way and then introduce some strategies so you can do something about it.

How you can sabotage your success

People struggle to have a success mindset for many reasons. In this chapter, I'll explore some of these which include:

- The impact of the media and television
- Other people's opinions and ideas
- Fraud or imposter syndrome
- Fear

- Emotional intelligence
- Your money mindset

Let's look at these different ways that you can sabotage yourself and what you can do about each one.

The impact of the media and television

The impact of the media and other negative news can affect the way you think. Ultimately, negative stories sell. As much as the news about the recession and economy is very real, the impact of this on your business has far-reaching effects. If you think about it, people make money and lose money in both buoyant and challenging times. I remember hearing some statistics from fellow coach, Tim Fearon from the *Extraordinary Coaching Company*, at a training course. He shared the statistics of wealth in the population. These indicate that:

- 1% are seriously wealthy
- 4% are wealthy
- 15% are doing well
- 60% are getting by
- 20% are struggling

These statistics don't change even when there is an economic crisis. I believe that much of your success comes down to your mindset, so if you believe the media, that will hugely impact on your business success.

As well as the news, we are also affected by the programmes we watch on television and the stories they portray. Often, the more dramatic the programme, the more viewers it will attract.

With this in mind, be careful about what you read and watch. If you develop the mindset of lack and negativity, this is what you are likely to get (think back to the vicious and virtuous circles I mentioned in the previous chapter).

Other people's opinions and ideas

Other people's opinions, ideas, fears and anxieties can also play a part in your motivation to succeed. As much as your family and friends are well meaning, their thoughts, attitudes and philosophies can impact on your mindset and approach. They have our best intentions at heart but, to be frank, how they tell us about these intentions does not always serve us. I reflect now on a current client who is in business and she wants to make it work, yet her friends are advising her to go back to a job that she does not want to do. This means that her focus on the task in hand, i.e. building her business, is thwarted by the worry and anxiety that this then creates.

In the late Jim Rohn said, 'You are the average of the five people you spend the most time with.' With this in mind, it makes sense to have the right people in your life – people who validate your choices and support you. That's not to say that you ignore those less supportive friends and family, or get rid of them from your life, but perhaps you choose to spend your time with others who inspire you, motivate you and make you feel good about yourself.

In saying that, it is not always others that get in the way of your success. As I inferred above, you may find that you do a pretty good job of doing this yourself!

Fraud syndrome

Fraud or imposter syndrome is a common way in which many people sabotage their success. Interestingly enough, up to 70% of people fear that they will be labelled as a phoney at some stage in their life. That's not to say that they are a phoney; perhaps something prevents them from believing how good they really are at their craft.

- They may think they are no good at something, despite their knowledge, experience or training
- They may be waiting for someone to find out that they are not as good as they say they are, even if deep down they know that they are good at what they do
- They may dismiss their accomplishments and successes as a stroke of luck, fluke, or a coincidence rather than basking in their success

If you face fraud syndrome, you will be more inclined to shy away from what you really want to do. Think back to the vicious and virtuous circles I talked about in the last chapter. If you are aware that you are feeling this way, this is a great time to take stock and work out how you can create a winning mindset for your business. Concentrate on the things that have gone well; surround yourself with people who empower you; approach your business with a renewed sense of purpose and passion; and hold onto positive thoughts and make the right decisions.

Fear

Fear is another thing that can stop people from being successful. I talked about your comfort zone before, and as much as fear can be a tangible reason for not doing something, I suggest that you can feel the fear and do it anyway.

The word fear can be defined as:

- An unpleasant emotion caused by the belief that someone or something is dangerous, likely to cause pain, or a threat
- A mixed feeling of dread and reverence
- A feeling of anxiety concerning the outcome of something or the safety and well-being of someone
- The likelihood of something unwelcome happening

You may have heard the acronym FEAR as having other definitions too, such as False Expectations Appearing Real. Fear is something that often paralyses us when we have no real belief that what we worry about is actually going to happen. When you are in this situation and are worrying about something, think about this: What is the worst that can happen? What is the best that can happen? It is what we tell ourselves about these fears that can stop us achieving the success we really want to have.

One of the best strategies for overcoming fear is by doing something that scares you or something that empowers you. I recently ran a workshop where the participants did a board break. If you've not done or come across a board break before, this is what happens. You have a piece of pine board, about 10 x 12 inches and 1 inch thick, and you write down your fears or the things you want to break through on one side of the board. Then on the other side of the board, you write the things that you really want to achieve (your goals and aspirations). Once you have done that, with the help of a trained instructor, you are taught how to physically break through the board with your bare hand. This creates a metaphor to help you to break through what is holding you back in your life or your business. I found this to be extremely powerful and motivating for everyone who did it. I'm also a Firewalk Instructor, and there is nothing more powerful than walking on red hot coals to really make you change the way you think about things!

Let me share with you a few truths about fears and some tips that will help you to manage them:

- Fear and anxiety are normal – they sharpen the senses
- Everyone feels fear and anxiety when they are on unfamiliar ground
- Fear and anxiety will never go away as you continue to grow, stretch your comfort zone and do something new
- The only way to resolve fear is to just do it
- Handling the fear is often less of an energy drain than worrying about something
- When you've handled the fear and achieved something, you will feel amazing!

Ten ways to manage fears

1. Manage your state. Your state can impact on how you feel and the actions you take. You can change your state by being aware of how you are feeling and doing something about it.
2. Change your posture and physiology. You can change the way you feel by changing your stance. Think about this – how do you sit or stand if you are in a negative state? How do you sit or stand if you are in a positive state?

What is the difference between the two? Also, motion changes your emotion, so by moving and doing something else can change the way you feel.

3. Manage your breathing. When you are fearful, there is a likelihood that you are breathing shallowly. So take the time to breathe from the diaphragm to get the oxygen you need to make the right decision.

4. Use your peripheral vision. You may find that when you are in a fearful state you have a narrow focus. Peripheral vision is a part of your vision that occurs outside the very centre of your gaze. Without focusing on anything in particular, look straight ahead and as you do this pay attention to what you notice out of the corners of both eyes simultaneously. When you use your peripheral vision, it helps to open up the conscious mind to other possibilities and removes tension.

5. Be aware of the power of your language. What you say to yourself influences your results. If you question your ability to do something, you are less likely to achieve it than if you are positively focused on results.

6. Manage your subconscious mind. It is not just what you say that affects your results. Your subconscious mind accepts things that you tell it, whether they are true or false. If you tell yourself you are weak it will accept it as true, and if you tell yourself you are strong, this will be accepted instead.

7. Manage your self-talk. Many of us have internal chatter, which may be positive or negative. As stated previously, positive self-talk makes us more resourceful and happier. The words we use to tell ourselves things impacts how we

feel. You have a choice on what your self–talk says to you, the language it uses and how what you think affects your life.

8. Frame or reframe situations. If you are faced with a negative situation, event or thought, you have the ability to frame or reframe these experiences. It is about seeing it differently and changing the message that you send to your brain.

9. Use affirmations. Affirmations are a powerful way to change your thought processes. A good affirmation has various facets: it is positive, stated in the present tense, and personal to you.

10. Expand your comfort zone. I touched on this previously. By stretching your comfort zone, you will be able to overcome your fears and be able to achieve greater results in your business.

If you don't learn how to handle your fears, it is going to be hard to break through and achieve your goals. It is time to change your own beliefs and achieve the results that you want in your life and your business.

What can you do differently?

We are all programmed in different ways and what we once felt can be changed. It is possible to break out of the negative patterns that no longer serve you or that you had in the past. If you want to do something differently you have two choices, one is to stay where you are and the other is to do it. You do have a choice as to how you feel every day when you get out of bed and if you do want to take action, you just need to develop the strategies to turn it around. I remember reading once that President Clinton said to

Nelson Mandela, 'How do you forgive your jailers?' and Mandela said, 'When I walked out of the gate I knew that if I continued to hate these people I was still in prison.'

Your emotional intelligence

Your emotional intelligence is a key part to cutting the crap, as the more emotionally intelligent you are, the more self aware you will be. You will be aware of the negative messages that you face and learn how to turn them around. You will recognise the beliefs that limit you and do something about them.

If you think about an iceberg, 80-90% of this is under water, and you just see a fraction of the structure. The same applies to humans. Much of why we do what we do is driven by the subconscious. The small amount of what you see is conscious – your skills and knowledge – and below the surface are your values, beliefs, motives and traits, which drive you and influence what you do. This is why having a high level of emotional intelligence is essential for your success.

There are various definitions of emotional intelligence, and should you wish to find out more, I suggest you read Daniel Goleman's books on this subject.

Emotional intelligence is about:

- Knowing how you and others feel and what to do about it
- Knowing what feels good and what feels bad and how to get from bad to good
- Possessing emotional awareness, sensitivity and the management skills that will help you to maximise your long-term happiness and survival

It is about understanding your intrapersonal and interpersonal skills to be successful. Intrapersonal skills constitute the inner intelligence you use to know, understand and motivate yourself; the ability to know understand and motivate yourself and be self-aware. Interpersonal skills include the ability to read, sense, understand, and manage your relationships with others as well as the ability to build rapport, motivate, influence and get on well with others. All of these are important in developing and running a successful business:

- If you know yourself and understand others, it helps you to master the effect you have on those around you
- People with a higher level of emotional intelligence are likely to have lower levels of stress, be able to build more effective relationships and get better outcomes
- You will understand your personal style, your impact on others, and how you can adapt this to get better results
- You will know your strengths and weaknesses, be open to feedback and development, and play to your strengths each day
- You will be aware of how you communicate, your energy levels, and how you can best manage yourself to get the most out of what you do

In his book, *Working with Emotional Intelligence*, Daniel Goleman says, 'For leadership positions, emotional intelligence competencies account for up to 85% of what sets outstanding managers apart from the average.' So this indicates why and how this is important in business.

Your money mindset

I talked about money a short while ago when I mentioned that the influence of the media can affect how successful you are in business, and the statistics of whether people make or lose money doesn't tend to change according to the economic climate.

Yet your money mindset can make or break your business. If you believe that your money mindset is limiting you, find yourself a Money Coach to help you to break through a ceiling that is holding you back, help you to focus on wealth and abundance rather than lack, and remove the blocks that may stop you from achieving your potential in business.

Moving onto step 5

Before we move onto step 5, I'd like to introduce one more exercise for you to do. I believe that when you are clear about what you want, it makes it easier to have the confidence to take action and to cut the crap. The problem is that many people don't really know what they want, where their real passion lies and the thing that they love to do. We will explore your expertise fully in the next chapter. Before that, I'd like to challenge you to put this book down. Take a couple of pieces of A4 paper and give yourself 10-15 minutes to do this exercise thoroughly.

What are your passions and talents?

On the first piece of paper, I would like you to write down your passions. What do you love to do? These are the things that will get you out of bed in the morning that you may have explored in the vision chapter.

On the second piece of paper, I would like you to write down your talents. What are you good at naturally? These are the things that you do naturally without thinking and may not even recognise them as talents because they seem easy to you.

Put both pieces of paper in front of you. Then I would like you to ask yourself this question: 'How do they go together?'

The sheet listing your passions will highlight the things that you love to do, and the other sheet will show your talents, knowledge, training and experience. You may or may not see how they can fit together. If not, don't choose one over the other; just know that there is a way in which they can work together, just by knowing that they exist.

Chapter 6
Step 5: Explore your expertise

'There is one quality which one must possess to win, and that is definiteness of purpose, the knowledge of what one wants, and a burning desire to possess it.'
– Napoleon Hill

You will have arrived at where you are today as a result of your background, your experience, and your knowledge. This will have shaped the life you have had, the jobs you have done, and what you have created for yourself to date. So, does it not make sense that you draw on this knowledge and experience in your business? It doesn't mean that you need to do exactly what you used to do, as you may have decided to set up a business to get away from your job, but you can probably find elements that you like and use them in your business. If you did the exercise in the last chapter, you will be well on track to doing this well.

The first step in exploring your expertise is to find out what you love to do (and also what you hate!).

Understanding your strengths

In Chapter 3, I suggested that you do a SWOT analysis for your business. It is an important thing to do in order to understand what you are good at and what you don't or can't do. It will shape your business development, affect what you outsource and ultimately what you get known for as a solopreneur. If you missed the exercise or didn't concentrate on focusing on you and your business, it is time to do this now.

Your strengths will clearly define the specialism you choose and the clients you work with. When you play to your strengths, it makes it easier to get clients, and you can do what you love. Even if you are a coach (and coaching is traditionally non-directive), your clients will often be looking for help from people with an expertise in solving their problems. Consider what you are good at and how this impacts on your business.

More than a niche

A niche is when you focus on working with a particular group of people. I'm sure that many of you have been told that you need to niche to be successful. You know that you need to find a hungry crowd, have a product or service that meets their needs, and be an expert. I often see people who have decided to niche, but it hasn't been narrow or deep enough to be truly successful. I've also seen others who are loathe to niche as they believe that, in doing so, they are restricting their client base.

If you are a generalist in your business, you are less likely to get results. That's not always the case as some people will get known as a result of their personality or due to the longevity of their business, but for many people, when they choose to become an expert, they get better and more consistent results.

My opinion is that you can't make money as a generalist life coach (and if you think about the 80/20 rule, this will translate to other professions) and the deeper you specialise, the easier it becomes. The problem is that I believe that it is no longer enough to niche. Using the coach example, you may say that you are a 'Career Coach' or that you solve a particular type of problem, but still people don't really understand what you do.

To be successful, you have to do more than just 'niching' – you need to have a clear notion of your ideal client, what their problems are and how you can help them, which I am going to be covering in this chapter. The easiest way to get business is through referrals and recommendations when people 'get' what you do, so it's important that you are clear about this yourself!

In addition, I find that solopreneurs are moving away from the traditional type of 'niching' and are matching their passion to their talents to find the thing they love to do.

Ultimately, it is a crowded marketplace out there and more people are giving up their day job, being made redundant and deciding to set up as a solopreneur, so you need to do something different to stand out from the crowd and get noticed.

Being an expert

Many years ago, I came across the *Pyramid of power and profit,* penned by Dan Kennedy and it transformed the way I thought about my business. It made me realise that what I was doing was not getting consistent results and I made significant changes to my business. It is a model I share with my clients regularly as it makes perfect sense, although I have put my own mark on the system. This is my interpretation of the pyramid to help you to get more clients and profit in your business.

There are 5 levels to my pyramid and if you think back to the 80/20 rule and business success, very few people make it towards the top of the pyramid and achieve the success they desire:

Generalist – this is the bottom level of the pyramid.

Most people in business are generalists. Using the coaching example, if you are a generalist, you will be a life coach. You will be offering your services to anyone and helping them with anything. You'll be trying to be all things to all people, but not have a clear specialism, let alone a clear idea of your ideal client. Ultimately, you will struggle to achieve success. The main problem is that your offering may be fluffy, indescribable and no one will understand what you really do.

Specialist – when you have decided to niche, this is where you are initially likely to be. You will have a specialism and can communicate this to people. They will have more of an understanding of what you do and the results you give your clients. But your niche does need to be clearly defined and communicated and it also needs to be something that people want. If you are a coach, you are likely to call yourself something like a career coach or relationship coach.

True specialist – this level was not in the original model, but it is an important factor in success. When you are a true specialist, you concentrate specifically on helping a certain group of people with a particular problem. It is more than just being a career coach; it may be about helping people with 'stress at work', 'cope with redundancy' or 'helping accountants to be better leaders'.

Expert – this is the next section in the pyramid and people generally reach this level when they have created a specialist programme, have had a book published, or speak extensively on stage. They are recognised as an expert or go-to-person in a particular field (i.e. they do something that makes them stand out from the crowd). Thinking about the pyramid, as you may imagine, there are fewer people in each level as you move up towards the top.

Celebrity – this is the top level. Examples of people in this area are Paul McKenna, Anthony Robbins,

Michael Neill; people who are perceived as celebrities in their field and are regularly in the media, charge high fees, and can sell out venues.

- Where in the pyramid would you position you and your business right now?
- Are you niched specifically enough?
- Where do you want to be?
- What will it take to get there?

In saying all of this, it's more than just the label you give yourself; it is also about the results you give to your clients. So let's move on to focusing on your ideal type of client.

Being an expert in your business

When you are an expert in your business, it makes it easier to get clients. People know what you do, who you work with and how you can help them. It also makes it easier for people to refer business to you. Isn't this the place you would like to be? The place where business is easy and effortless rather than difficult and painful?

When you have decided in which area to specialise, the next step is to think about the people with whom you would like to work. For example, let me take you back to the career coach example. If you decide to specialise as a career coach, what is your true specialism? Perhaps you decide to work with 'stress at work'. This potential niche is still a broad area and there are a couple of questions to ask before you proceed. Who do you want to work with within this niche? Who is your ideal client?

It is important to identify the people you want to work with as these are the people you will be spending your time with every day.

Know your ideal client

There are various reasons to know your ideal client:

1. It helps you to determine where to find potential clients who are looking for the service which you offer. You will know where to concentrate your marketing efforts and make sure that you provide an offering that is compelling and well received by your clients.
2. You will know what your clients do every day, what they read and where they go.
3. You will know how to find them and what marketing techniques are likely to work.
4. You will get a reputation in the industry for the results you give to your clients.
5. You will be able to define your ideal client within this market – someone who you love to work with.
6. You will be able to develop a signature system that your clients will love (but more about that later).

It doesn't mean that you can't work with anyone else; you will just have a clear picture of the type of person you want to work with and then the transformation you can offer them (but more on this later).

To enable you to identify your ideal client, a good place to start is by looking at the clients that you work with at the moment (if you already have a business).

It makes sense to work with clients that you love to work with. Don't you want to work with people who inspire you rather than drain you? It may help to define the type of person you don't enjoy working with first as this will help you to define your ideal client. To begin to identify the types of clients you don't want, consider what characteristics and behaviours you refuse to tolerate. What turns you off or shuts you down? What kind of client do you not want to work with?

Take a look at your current clients and be absolutely honest with yourself. Are you already working with any people with these characteristics? If this is the case, what are you going to do about it?

Who are your best clients right now? What is it about their characteristics, qualities and behaviours that you like?

If you don't already run a business, what type of client would you love to work with? Consider these people when you answer the questions above.

Your ideal client

In the last section we looked at who you would like to work with and your best and worst clients, so now is the time to get into the detail. To recap, when you work with your ideal clients, you will:

- Have the energy to do your best work
- Feel invigorated and inspired
- Connect with your clients on a deeper level
- Feel successful and confident

Your ideal client exercise

It's time to do some thinking. Get a clear picture of your ideal client in your head. Write down the 5 main reasons why you love working with them.
1.
2.
3.
4.
5.

Now is the time to get really specific. Give your ideal client an avatar – a name and create a picture so that you are clear about who they are and where you can find them.

What gender is your ideal client? (You are not allowed to say both unless you work with couples).

How old are they? Be as specific as you can within a 5–10 year range.

What distinguishing family features do they have? Are they single, married, partnered? Do they have children or elderly relatives that they are caring for?

Where do they live? Be as specific as you can.

What do they do for a living? Or are they in school, in college, out of work or retired? Be as specific as you can in terms of their occupation.

What do they do when they are not working? (If they work.)

What do they do when they are not busy? Where do they go? Who do they spend their time with?

If you work with corporations, these questions may not be so relevant, but they may help you to define the types of people within organisations you would like to work with. If this is the case, here are some additional questions for you:

What type of organisation is your ideal company?

What sector are they in?

How many employees do they have?

What distinguishing features do they have (this may include problems they face)?

Where are they located?

Is there anything you need to think about when defining this person or organisation?

I hope you have taken the time to answer these questions. I know it can be hard to be specific, but the closer you get to your ideal client, the easier it is to find them. For example, when you do your elevator pitch at networking events, you can tell people about your ideal client and I'm sure that many of them will know this person and then be able to tell them about you. If you are general and say that you work with anyone, solving anything, what do you think will happen next? In case you are wondering, I'll be talking more about how you can do an effective elevator pitch later.

When I initially set up my business, my true specialism was working with people facing career change and redundancy to help them to find a job that they love. This made people realise the types of people I worked with. But this wasn't enough on its own. My ideal client is a lady, who I called 'Sarah'. She is 39, in a professional role, with a family and partner. This means that she works full time, has a busy life with the children and not much time for herself. Remember Sarah because in a moment I'll expand on this further. In the meantime, I would like to introduce you to the next concept in exploring your expertise.

It is not enough to know the basic details when it

comes to understanding your ideal clients. In knowing who they are enables you to do the next bit with ease. What are your clients' problems?

What are your clients' problems?

Everyone has problems, including your clients. Now you have identified who your clients are, what problems do they have that may trigger them to pick up the phone to talk to you?

Let me suggest an exercise for my creative readers. Take a piece of paper and draw a picture of your ideal client – a stick person will do. Think about the types of problems they may have:

- What are they thinking?
- What are they saying to themselves?
- What are they saying to others?

Then draw thought bubbles and speech balloons to express this on the paper. Remember to use their language based on the person or avatar you created in the last section.

For example, using the career example and Sarah above, she may be thinking, 'I'm fed up with having no time for me.' She may be saying, 'I hate my job but don't have time to find a new one,' and she may be saying to others, 'My life isn't going the way I planned.' Be free with your thoughts, and if you are struggling, find someone you know who could be your ideal client and ask them about their problems!

How can you help your clients?

When you know the problems that your clients face, it is easier to look at how you can help them or ultimately the transformation that you can provide.

Take a few moments now to look at some of the problems you identified above. What solutions or transformations can you offer your clients?

Your potential client is going to want to know what is in it for them to work with you. How can you make their life better? What pain, problem or difficulty will your service help or eliminate?

One of the most important secrets in business is that clients don't buy the service you provide. They don't buy coaching, they don't buy a massage, and they don't buy a management training course. But … they do buy the results that they get when they receive that service, which is why I am urging you to do this now. They buy the promise of getting a job they will love, the feeling they will get when the knots in their shoulders have melted away, and the improvement they see in the leadership skills of their management team.

You have to know both their pain and the solutions you provide to enable your prospective clients to understand what you do and this in turn, facilitates the next steps in this process.

Before I move on to this stage – identifying the features and benefits of your service – let me briefly take you back to Sarah.

Sarah wants to find a job that she will love. She may not care much about the process that is used to get there; she just needs to trust that you can facilitate that journey and that you have the expertise to help her. She wants to know about other people who you have helped so she can be assured that you can give her similar results.

What are the features and benefits of your service?

Many people get confused by the difference between features and benefits. They then try to sell the features of what they do rather than the benefits that they offer. I touched on this earlier by asking you how you can help your clients. At this point, I would like to go into a little more detail and give you a short exercise to complete.

The features of your products and services can be defined as follows:

- A distinctive attribute or aspect of something
- A factual statement about the product or service being promoted

A feature will tell a client about the number of sessions and how you work with them. The reason that a feature can be confused with a benefit is that some of the benefits you think you offer will in fact be features of what you do!

Let's look at the features of a career coaching programme. A feature could be that the programme offers the individual a review of their CV. You may think that a benefit of this will be that your client will have a CV that gets them interviews in their chosen field. However, in reality, this is just an extension of the original feature. What is the true benefit of this CV review?

- It may be that they will have the confidence to approach new employers
- It may be that they will feel happier about their skills and abilities to do a different job
- It may be that they trust that they will find a job

they will love
- It may be that they will feel happier and more content with their life

These are still pretty much high-level features and benefits, but I hope that you are starting to see the bigger picture.

Let's look at benefits in a little more detail. A benefit can be defined as:

- Something that entices a customer to buy
- The advantage of something
- What's in it for the customer
- The value for the customer and how you can enhance their lives

Just think ... 'People don't want to buy a quarter-inch drill, they want a quarter-inch hole,' said Theodore Levitt. People don't buy glasses; they buy better vision and a stylish look. People don't buy a new dress; they buy the amazing feeling they get when they wear it out on a date.

Therefore, people don't buy what you are offering; they buy a result, an outcome or a transformation. And this will often be based on emotion, and how you can make their life better.

So why don't you try this for yourself?

Features exercise

Make a list of the features of one of your services or products.

Feature 1:

Feature 2:

Feature 3:

Feature 4:

Feature 5:

For 3 of the best features you have identified, work with a partner to establish the benefits of these features by asking the other person the following question after each benefit they have identified:

What will that give them?

Continue asking this question until you have identified 10 benefits of each feature and record your answers below.

Feature 1:

Benefits of feature 1:

Feature 2:

Benefits of feature 2:

Feature 3:

Benefits of feature 3:

Brilliant! I hope that by now you have a clearer idea of what you do, how you do it and why your clients need it.

As I touched on earlier, it can make your life much easier as you can tell people what you do, thus attracting more clients. When you love what you do, you'll be passionate about your business and what you do every day, so doesn't this all make sense?

To go back to Sarah – in defining your ideal client, it doesn't mean that, in this example, that you only work with 39-year-old women. It doesn't stop you working with Ian, a 38-year-old man who wants to change his career, or Rebecca, a lady in her early 40s who doesn't know whether to stay self-employed or find a new job, or Jim, a gentleman in his 60s who doesn't know what to do next after being made redundant. What it does is to help you to focus on how you market your business, to whom you write your marketing copy and how you find your ideal clients, which is coming up now.

Moving onto step 6

Look at the information we've covered so far. When you started this process, you may have felt that you were limiting yourself when you focus on who you want to work with, when in fact you are opening up to doing what you really wanted to do when you set up your business in the first place. This helps you to target your ideal client, perfect your pitch, and get clear on your website and so much more. Remember you can download all the exercises and additional tips at www. HowToStandOut.co.uk.

Chapter 7
Step 6: Sculpt your marketing plan

'The will to win, the desire to succeed, the urge to reach your full potential ... These are the keys that will unlock the door to personal excellence.'
– Eddie Robinson

The information and exercises that you have completed throughout this book so far will have set you up for this point, which is when you start to find out more about your clients and market your services to them. There are many things to cover and many people make the mistake of not covering each of the steps. This means that they create their website before they know what their business actually does, and this can result in major changes (and increased costs) later on. Or, they change their message every time they go to a networking meeting, which results in people not understanding what they actually do.

In this chapter, I shall go through some of the steps you can follow to sculpt your marketing plan and then, importantly, get sales. If you have completed the exercises in this book, you will have a clearer idea of your ideal client, what they do and where you can find them, which is essential for this stage. Many people, when they think of marketing, do everything that they could do and this causes sub-standard results. I believe that you should choose 3 different types of marketing activities, and when you do them well and with mastery, you will accelerate your results.

Simply marketing is 'the action or business of promoting and selling products or services' or 'the process responsible for identifying, anticipating and satisfying customer requirements profitably'.

As already mentioned, the main difference in marketing for many of you is that you are not selling a product, but selling yourself as a service, which puts a different complexion on your marketing activities. People are buying something which is intangible and they can't automatically see how it works, which means that you need to do something different. Even if you have products as part of your service, the number one key to marketing is through building relationships and creating a unique strategy that works well for your business.

I touched on this briefly in *The Secrets of Successful Coaches*, but it would be prudent to mention the marketing mix here as it is relevant to this step. There are four main **P**s to the marketing mix:

Product – You need to have a tangible product or service. This will include your brand name, quality, type of service and how it is delivered. Whether this is a service or tangible product, you need to specify what this is to enable you to market your business.

Price – You will also need to know your price. This may be a pricing strategy dependent on different services or products, or a range of packages or programmes that you offer to your clients.

Place – This is important, as this is the action of getting the product or service to the customer. Therefore, you need to decide how you are going to provide the service to the customer, which may include one-to-one programmes, workshops, and e-books, among other ways.

Promotion – This is the final of the 4 **P**s which includes aspects of marketing your business including your promotional strategy, advertising, and other forms or marketing.

In addition, you need to have the right people in place, so this will include yourself and anyone who works with you. You need to have efficient processes in which to deliver this service or product, to ensure your client satisfaction, and finally, you need the physical evidence, which is about where, when and how you are delivering the service you are offering to your client.

Ultimately, marketing is about offering the right product to your client, at the right price, at the right time and in the right way.

Your products and services

Let's start in this section by looking at your products and services. To be successful in business, you need to have a range of products and services to offer your clients around your area of expertise. It is simply not enough to offer your one-to-one time for many reasons.

Firstly, there are only so many hours in every week and you can't spend all of this time with your clients. You need to allow time to market your business, develop your products and other things that you need to do to work 'on your business' rather than just 'in your business'. If you worked out how many hours you could work each year and times this number by your ideal hourly rate, how would this meet your income goals? Actually, stop and take a calculator out now and work this out.

For example, after holidays and public holidays, you will probably work around 45 weeks per year. If you had 10 clients a week and you charged £50 per session, you would be earning £22,500 a year. You could charge more money (which I would advocate for many of you), package up your services (more on that later), and work with more clients (but remember to leave time for marketing, networking and building relationships). So, wouldn't it be useful to have multiple streams of income allowing you to make money whilst you sleep and have different ways to bring money into your business?

Secondly, not every client will be ready and willing to work with you on a one-to-one basis, without experiencing more of what you do first. Perhaps a different solution would work better anyway.

I would like to introduce you to the marketing funnel. Some people say that this process is a bit outdated, but I do believe that it is a good way to show how you can organise your products and services.

Many clients will find you as a result of your marketing, so it is important to get your promotional tools right (more about these later), but before you can promote you, you need to get your funnel into place.

Most people will enter your marketing funnel because of a freebie that you offer them. In the personal development industry, this tends to be in the form of a free report, audio, workbook or something else of value (and it must be your best stuff!) that you provide to a prospective client. Most people will have this freebie on their website and give it away in exchange for the prospect's name and email address, where they will normally opt into your list. This also may be as a result of speaking at an event, exhibiting at a show, a free teleseminar, or another way in which you have captured a prospect's personal details. Another way of someone entering your funnel is through you offering a free introductory session to them.

Having told them how you can help them, this client may decide to buy from you. As I mentioned earlier, it is not enough to sell just your one-to-one time, so a range of options at different price points is good practice. This makes up your marketing funnel.

What types of products could you have? Here are a few ideas for you, which are broken down into 5 different price points:

Freebie:
Report or workbook
Video series
Audio recording
Teleseminar or webinar

Low investment:
Book or e-book
Membership club
Masterclass

Medium investment:
Group programme
Telesummit or interview series
Workshops or events
Online workshop or programme

Higher investment:
One-to-one programmes
Retreats

VIP:
VIP programme
Group mastermind programme

What products and services do you or could you offer at each level?

Freebie:

Low investment:

Medium investment:

High investment:

VIP:

I hope that you have at least one or two ideas for each level and you may have put an investment cost for each product or service.

A word of caution here. Don't complete this stage until you have found out what your customer wants and that they will buy these products from you. I have seen and heard of plenty of situations where solopreneurs have spent many hours putting together new and shiny products, yet no one wants to buy them. So make sure that there is a market for your product before you spend the time developing it. Believe me, I know as I've done it myself – and learnt from my mistakes!

One more point on this – it's not necessary to have all your products and services up and running when you start your business. They will develop as you grow your business and you find out more about what your client wants from you. With this in mind, let's find out more about your client.

Do your market research

You will now have an idea of who your ideal clients are, their problems and some of the solutions you provide. Think about what you would like to find out about your clients. You might want to find out more about their problems. You might also want to test out whether they are interested in your products or services, as there is not much point in having a niche where people don't want to buy.

Once you know what you want to find out, choose a way to get this information. There are various options. You could hold a focus group with your ideal clients, you could invite a person in your target market for a coffee and a chat, or you could do a survey or questionnaire. All of these are easy and valid ways to find out about people in your target market and find out what they want. It you choose the latter, look at a survey tool such as www.surveymonkey.com as this is a great way to collate your questions and then review your answers. Just make sure you start with the end in mind and ask the right questions.

Survey tips

Let me share with you a few tips about carrying out surveys:

1. Give people an incentive to complete the questionnaire – you could give away some of your time, a prize draw of one of your products or something else that your audience will benefit from. Tell them about this in a short summary before you start the questions. You may also choose to capture their name and contact details and follow up with them later (with their permission of course).
2. Ask a mixture of different types of questions. Get quantitative results by asking questions that require your respondents to tick boxes, as this will give you statistics and numbers (avoid too many options). You will also get qualitative results by asking for their comments using open questions. This will give you a real insight into your client's thoughts, language and problems.
3. Make it easy for people to complete. Tell them

how long it will take them to complete and why they should do it.
4. Test your survey with a friend or a colleague to make sure that the questionnaire works, that the questions are logical, and make sure you proofread it.
5. Give people a chance to add other comments. These are invaluable as you can find out what people really think in their own words.
6. Ask people to share your survey so you can get a good response. Send it out to your list, share it on social media, and ask others to do the same.
7. Do something with your research. Produce a summary for respondents, blog about the results, start to produce the products your clients want and ultimately make sure you act on the information!

Another way to do some research is by finding out more about your competitors. Who are they? What do they do?

It is good to have competitors, because if other people are doing well in your industry and niche, you are more likely to do the same. If you don't have any competitors, I suggest you ask yourself two questions: 1. 'Is this because I have managed to identify a niche before anyone else has identified this need?' 2. 'Is this because there is no market for my product or service?'

When you have taken the time to identify your competitors, discover what they are doing and what works for them. Personally, I don't see people in a similar profession to me as being a competitor as I believe there is more than enough space for all of us. We are not all going to be the ideal coach, consultant, etc., for every client who contacts us and we are all unique in our products, services, and way of working.

Just remember to use the information you get and take action. For example, if your clients are saying their problems are in getting their CV noticed, produce a free report to show them how to do it. You could also run a 'Get Your CV Noticed' masterclass via teleseminar or webinar, or perhaps you could hold a CV workshop. As much as this may feel counter-intuitive, don't produce paid-for products until people have signed up for the programme. You don't want to waste your time creating something that people don't want. Even if they say they want it, it isn't the same as them completing a bank transfer or a PayPal payment!

Different ways to market your services

There are a hundred and one different ways to market your business and it is not possible to cover every single variable in this book. However, I can give you some dos and don'ts based on my experience and leave you to make your own decisions.

Your choice of which way to market your business is also going to change and develop as your business grows, which I will share towards the end of this chapter. In this section, I will share with you some of the most common ways in which you can market your business and increase your client base.

Networking and your perfect pitch

As I mentioned earlier in the book, the best way for service-based solopreneurs to get business is through building relationships with other people. Despite the age of social media and online networking (coming next), you can't just sit behind your computer. You have to get out and meet others!

The most common way of building relationships in

business is through networking. Briefly, networking is the process of interacting with others to exchange information or experiences for mutual benefit. There are many ways in which you can network to build your business, get clients and become known for what you do. It is also a great opportunity to meet referral partners, contacts who can help you in business and make friends with people. It can be a lonely business working for yourself!

There are various types of networking groups from informal coffee shop get-togethers to formal breakfast meetings. The first thing you need to do is find the right networking events for you. When you know who your ideal client is, it makes life much easier, as this is likely to influence your choice of networking group. For example, if you want to speak with business owners, you'll find that mums' groups are less likely to be effective, but if your target audience is female business owners with children, this will be a great place to start. On the other hand, networking is more than just meeting your ideal client. When you have your message clear, these people are more likely to be able to refer you to their colleagues and friends, as they will understand what you do and how you can help them.

Some networking groups will allow you to try before you buy, and others will offer a pay per session charge. Ask people you already know in business. Where do they go? What do they do? Check out the trade journals or search on the Internet to find groups in your area. Before you make a huge investment, make sure that the network group you choose is the right one for you and that it will give you the right returns. Some networking groups allow you to come along as a guest for a while without obligation to sign up. This type of opportunity will help you decide what's best for you.

When you choose the right group, you'll meet

with like-minded people, build effective business and personal relationships, and, of course, promote your business. When you attend consistently and regularly, people will get to know you. As well as talking about you, you'll also be referring others to your connections.

With this in mind, it is worth sharing some networking tips. Remember that first impressions count and that people will be making an impression of you within the first few seconds of meeting you.

One of the mistakes that many business owners make when introducing themselves at networking events is by introducing themselves by their profession, e.g. a coach, massage therapist, etc. With the former, this will invoke a number of responses; some people will be thinking, 'Not another coach!' Others will ask you, 'What sport?' and some won't have a clue what you do. The trick is to put together your elevator pitch, which is so named as it is the short introduction you can carry out in the time span of a ride in a lift or elevator. It is good practice to have a short sentence you can share when talking to someone on a one-to-one introductory basis, and a one-minute pitch when you have an opportunity to introduce yourself formally to a group of people.

Before I move on, let's take some time to consider your perfect pitch.

Your perfect pitch

Who are you?

What do you do? (In one short sentence)

What are 3 results you give to your clients?

1.

2.

3.

Who are you looking for?

One of the other big mistakes made with networking is to miss out on potential opportunities. You'll be going to networking events to meet new people and to build relationships, so it is important not to go away with a bunch of business cards and then file them in a drawer somewhere. Follow-up is essential.

If you think you will forget who you meet, when you take someone's business card, make a few notes on the back, e.g., where you met them and what you talked about. It will help your memory later. Then follow up with people after the event so you don't miss out on any potential opportunities. Keep in touch with them; a simple personal email or telephone call won't take you long and who knows where it might lead?

One-to-one meetings

Networking is more than just going to networking groups. It is about sharing your message with the people you know and scheduling individual meetings. Start by talking to people you know. Who do you know already who can help you to promote your business? Perhaps you have contacts with ex-colleagues, friends, or friends of friends. If you want to meet a specific person, just ask someone you know, as we are all just a few steps away from the people we want to meet.

Secondly, when you meet people at networking events, take some time to find out more about them.

It's not about building a group of transient people you may see from time to time, it is about creating a network of supportive people. Invite them out to lunch or coffee and get to know them on a personal basis. This will give you a great opportunity to find out more about them, how you can work together, or help each other out.

Cold or warm calling

Another way of building relationships is via the telephone. Cold calling means speaking to people that you have never met before, and may often be after sending out a letter or direct mailing a group of prospective clients.

Warm calling means speaking to those who you have met at a networking event or someone who has expressed an interest in working with you (either directly or through a mutual contact). For service-based business owners, warm calling is easier to do as you already have a relationship with the person or a mutual contact, and this is a good way to further develop your relationship. In fact, instead of meeting a prospect for coffee, a virtual coffee over Skype or the phone works equally well.

How to build relationships

You will be building relationships with people each time you have contact with them, whether this is face-to-face, online or through something you have produced. Although I have shared some networking strategies, the trick is to be authentically your best you as you build relationships. You are your brand and showing you and your business in the best light possible is one of the secrets to success.

Online marketing

Marketing is not just limited to face-to-face meetings, telephone calls and networking. The worldwide web has meant that there has been a shift in the way we market ourselves and our businesses. I am referring to online marketing and when you think about this concept, you may just be thinking about your website, or a social media platform like Facebook. However, there is a plethora of tools that you can use to get your message across via the Internet. Let's look at some of these areas now.

Your website

Your website is likely to be one of the most important ways in which you build your business on the Internet. These days you don't have to spend thousands of pounds creating a website. There is a variety of platforms which make it easy for a web designer to develop a website that you can easily update, and that works well for you. I talked about this in more detail in Chapter 3.

These days, a good website for solopreneurs is not a static brochure site that people see and then call you. There is a lot of information on the web and people are short on time. You know that when you physically meet someone, that person will make a first impression of you within the first few seconds, and the same goes for your website.

It is important to capture your reader's attention within the first few seconds, and compel them to read on. Remember that the reason for your website is all about the client, not you, and make sure it is positioned in that way. For example, you could include a video, ask them some questions and tap into the reason they came across your website in the first place.

Let me introduce you to AIDA

AIDA is something you need to know about when you create your website and indeed any other marketing materials. AIDA stands for Attention, Interest, Desire, and Action:

Attention: The first thing you want to do with any marketing materials is to grab the reader's attention. You could do this with a great headline, question or image that makes them look twice at the information you are providing.

Interest: Then you need to keep their interest. So whatever you write, write it from the reader's viewpoint. Talk about the reader rather than yourself, share features and benefits, and keep it simple.

Desire: Through the words and images that you use, you want to be creating a desire and emotion in your reader to do something else. To create this desire, you could consider using testimonials, case studies, or facts and figures that make them think and want to do something about it.

Action: You have to tell your reader what to do next and this is where keeping it simple is so important. Do you want them to call you, fill in a form or send you an email? Just make sure you keep it to one 'call to action' per page as a confused mind never buys.

AIDA is important, and it is also vital to know the reason for your website, and what you want people to do when they land on one of your pages. The most successful coaches and solopreneurs build their list through their website by using one of the email marketing providers. They also have a blog where they regularly share useful articles, tips and strategies. I'll expand more on these strategies in a moment. In the meantime, here are my top tips to create your web copy, as well as making sure you remember AIDA.

Website strategies

- Don't talk about what you do, e.g. coaching; mention the problems you solve rather than how you do it
- Be clear about your ideal client and write with them in mind; talk to them directly
- Have a clear purpose for your website and tell people what you want them to do next
- A great way to do this is by providing a compelling reason for someone to opt-in to a freebie on your website, thus starting to create your all important database
- Share your story which prompted you to set up your business in the first place, and how this relates to the way you help your clients
- If you are not very good with words, find a good copywriter to help you. Your website may be the first place that people find out about you and your message needs to be compelling enough for people to get in touch with you
- To stand out from the crowd, have a video of you sharing your message as well as the text on the page
- Have a single call to action on each page. What

do you want the reader to do next? Do you want them to sign up to a free report, call you for a consultation, or something else?

List building

I have already mentioned the need to build a list or a community. In the personal development industry, at least, there is the adage that 'the money is in the list'. It is true that when you have a bona fide list of prospects, it makes it easier to develop and grow your business. In simple terms, a list is a group of people interested in your services.

The most effective way to grow your list is by signing up to an email marketing provider. There are plenty of options from free or low-cost versions like MailChimp, Icontact, ConstantContact and Aweber, to the more advanced (and expensive) systems like 1ShoppingCart and Infusionsoft. Be warned, it can be a false economy to go for the cheapest option at the early stages because if you later transfer your list to a different provider, there is a chance that you can lose some of your list when you do this – been there, done that!

Start by considering what you want the provider to do. If you want a system that is all singing all dancing, choose Infusionsoft which is the one used by many of the experts in the personal development industry, but naturally this is reflected in the monthly fee. If you want to integrate a shopping cart, you may want to consider 1ShoppingCart and, for a good all-round newsletter programme where you can create multiple lists, Aweber is a good choice. I advise you not to start to build your list through Outlook. It doesn't look professional and it is easy to forget to blind copy in your subscribers which can cause upset with your clients.

Remember that you need to focus on your ideal client and give them the information that they will want. Give them a reason to opt in to your list (this is your freebie that I mentioned earlier in this chapter) and make sure that this freebie gives the solution to one of their problems. For example, this may be the 'Get your CV Noticed' document mentioned earlier. It is no longer enough to expect people to sign up for a newsletter as we get bombarded with information every day, so give people regular value and what they want. You also need to share your best content, which shows you in your greatest light. If you give great information free of charge, what fabulous information you will give when people pay you for it!

If you are wondering what to share, start with top tips. Comment on recent news articles, link to notable events, tell people what you are doing in your business and how you can help them. Although there is a fine line, you don't want to inundate people with information, but you need to follow up regularly.

In the early days you may find that you have a few people on your list (and some may be your friends and family!), but in doing this you will get into the routine of keeping in touch. By the way, if you are not a writer and you find this daunting, choose something like a video message instead.

Remember you are building relationships here, so think about your list as a tribe who are interested in what you have to say. They are not just a 'list'; they are individual people with whom you want to share. When you have a list-building mindset, you will find that list building is not confined to your website. Find ways to organically grow your list. If you are speaking at an event, ask people if they would like your freebie. If you are at a networking event, ask people (the right ones!) whether they would like to opt in to get your information. Add your list opt-in form to your social media sites too. Just remember not to spam people!

Lastly, think quality not quantity. There are many people out there with thousands of people on their list and you don't have to be one of them unless you want to be! The important thing is to attract people who will benefit from you and buy your services. Numbers are not important but relationships are, so take time to cultivate and nurture the people on your list, provide valuable and educational information and encourage two-way communication and interaction.

Writing

If writing is something that you enjoy and are good at, make it part of your marketing strategy. It is easy to market your business by writing online and offline articles. From your newsletter to blogging, to creating ezine articles and getting published in the press, there are many choices available to you. You could also create an e-course or other online programmes, and post on forums relevant to your audience. Do your research and find the best way to market yourself using this skill.

One of the secrets to success in business is re-purposing the information that you create. For example, when you create a newsletter article, this can become a blog or an ezine article (or even a physical article, but more about that later). In creating this book, I have drawn on resources, tips, articles, webinars, and other information that I have produced for my clients over the years.

Social media

Social media is a very popular marketing tool and a great way to stand out from the crowd. Therefore, it is probably going to be an important part of your marketing strategy. Whatever way you market yourself, knowing your ideal client is important, because if they don't use social media, there is not much point in mastering any of these mediums. Like many forms of marketing, with social media you have a choice. In fact, you have many choices.

Social media is the use of web-based and mobile technologies to turn communication into interactive dialogue. There are many social media platforms available and they change on a daily basis. In this book, I will talk about the 3 main platforms and leave you to explore the rest at your convenience.

The main 3 that are used by individuals and businesses are Facebook, Twitter, and LinkedIn. Today, people are not just accessing social media via their computer, but are constantly using the platforms via their mobile phone and tablets.

Although many people use the platforms to maintain connections with family, friends and colleagues, share information, build relationships, and make new friends, they are increasingly enabling entrepreneurs to acquire new clients and make money in their business.

Think about it, you will probably connect on social media with people you have met at networking events. You may build relationships with mutual friends, and you will be sharing what you do each day.

Social media statistics

If you are not yet sure whether social media is for you, let me share some statistics with you (from 2010/11):

- 500 million people use Facebook on a regular basis and 250 million use it on a daily basis

- 75 million people use Twitter on a regular basis and 15 million are active users
- 65% of the world's top 100 companies have a Twitter account
- LinkedIn has 70 million users worldwide
- 100% of the Fortune 500 Company Directors are on LinkedIn
- 78% believe peers and 17% believe an advert

As well as the above example, as a solopreneur, there are various ways in which you can use social media. For example, you can get connected with those people with whom you would like to be in contact; you can do market research; you can create and build your online community; you can endorse others and get recommendations yourself; you can tell people what you do; you can engage with potential clients; you can share and promote events; you can tell people about your successes; you can ask questions, and ultimately, in doing all of this, you can build your online presence and brand.

Social media is more than sharing what you had for breakfast (and to be honest, if you are using social media for business, I would advise against doing this!).

You do need to consider which of the social media platforms will work for you and where your clients are likely to hang out. You will also need to consider your privacy, get some support and training, and learn from the experts how to make it work for you in business.

Let me share with you a few key tips about the different platforms.

Facebook tips:

- If you have a personal Facebook page, you can set up a Facebook page for your business
- You can have a Facebook button linking from your website and vice versa
- You can set up lists to manage your privacy which means that you can share different updates and information with personal and business contacts
- You can add your events, you can invite your Facebook friends to attend them and ask others to share them
- You can add an opt-in form to your Facebook page which enables people to easily sign up to your list
- You can set up secret, private or open groups where you can share information, which is a great way to build an exclusive public or private community
- You can also create targeted (paid-for) adverts to suggest people 'like' your page or to direct them to another web page enabling you to promote an event or product

Twitter strategies:

- Setting up a Twitter account is a quick and free way to get an online presence
- Use your name or business name when you sign up – people will get to know your business as a brand or you as a person
- You only have 140 characters to express your message so you need to be short and concise
- You can choose to follow people you find interesting and read their 'tweets'
- You can share and 're-tweet' any information

that you think your target audience will find useful, e.g. tweets from other businesses, relevant news, useful articles or information
- You can promote your business through Twitter using a mixture of informative tweets and those which promote your products or services. Just make sure you don't over-promote and under-share!
- You need to have a keyword specific profile so people can easily find you, for example sharing details about the people you work with and the benefits you provide

LinkedIn approaches:

- LinkedIn is mainly used for individual professional networking. You can set up a personal account for free
- As long as you set up your profile effectively, it gives other people a sense of who you are, your values and what you do
- To be most effective, share your current and past jobs, and education details
- Include a photo of yourself so this makes your profile more personal
- You can also set up a group for your business which you can invite people to join and share with their friends
- You can join groups which are relevant to your clients and share your knowledge and expertise
- You can ask people to personally recommend you through the endorsement link
- You can spend 5 minutes a day on LinkedIn and effectively use your time by updating your status – these may be things that your networks would find interesting about you that they don't already know!

Managing your social media

If you decide to use all of the social media platforms for your business, it is likely to feel overwhelming. So find the one that works best for you, even if you use the others to a lesser extent. Then have a plan and measure your results. It is easy to get distracted and lose valuable time when you start to use social media.

One of the secrets for managing your social media well is to use a platform such as Hootsuite or TweetDeck to connect your social media accounts and manage it effectively and efficiently. With Hootsuite, you can connect up to 5 accounts for free and schedule updates when you are away from the office. There is a caveat with this advice! All of the social media platforms are different in the way you communicate and the message you send, so don't automatically update all three platforms at one time with exactly the same message. In the same way that you communicate with people face-to-face, choose your message wisely, be consistent to your brand, and ultimately, let people get to know you and always be interested in others.

Using video

If you are thinking about using video for business, I'm sure the first word that comes to mind is YouTube. According to their website, 60 hours of video are uploaded every minute, and over 4 billion videos are viewed a day. In addition, over 800 million unique users visit YouTube each month and over 3 billion hours of video are watched each month. In 2011, YouTube had more than 1 trillion views, or almost 140 views for every person on Earth!

Wow, I'm sure you would agree that these are

pretty amazing statistics! If you are in the business of building relationships, what better way to get your message across online?

I know that creating videos is not going to be the natural marketing strategy for everyone reading this book. However, it is a very effective one. Whilst I'm not a video expert, I have produced professional and informal videos and generally know what works. You may choose to shoot a video as part of your sales copy for a new programme you are offering, have one on the front page on your website, or do short top tips or blog updates. As long as you know your clients and what they want, you are in a good starting place.

Video tips:

Get your lighting and background right – if you can't afford to go to a professional videographer, make sure your lighting and background is as good as can be. Although the content is the most important aspect, if the quality or background distracts people, it is easy for them to press the stop button.

Keep your videos short and to the point – I mentioned earlier that people generally have a short attention span. If you are providing excellent content, then people will be willing to watch, but for promotional videos, keep them short and succinct; about 60–90 seconds is ideal.

Create an outline script so you know what you want to say, but unless you have an autocue, be aware that you may not keep to each point. You might want to check out your message with colleagues and clients so you ensure you get the right points across.

Remember – benefits, benefits, benefits. Need I say more! Lastly, make sure you include a call to action. What do you want the person to do after he/she has watched your video? (Make sure it is just a single action or you could confuse them.)

Offline marketing

So far, in this section on marketing, I've been talking about relationship building, both face-to-face and via online marketing. As much as building relationships are great ways to build your business, that doesn't mean you should forget about offline or physical marketing materials, such as advertising, and promotional material, some of which will be used in tandem with relationship building anyway.

Advertising

If you are looking to get advertising in a mainstream publication that you believe your clients will read, you are looking at paying thousands of pounds in advertising fees, and I don't believe that you will recoup this investment. There are other options such as local directories and magazines, but again, think wisely before you spend your money.

Personally, I believe that advertising doesn't work, at least not for coaches, not unless you are prepared to invest in regular adverts over a period of time, and that you have the right message going out to clients. The only time I have seen it work is when it is combined with other methods of marketing. For example, you target an area with multiple forms of marketing. Perhaps you advertise in the local magazine, do a mail drop, get an article published in the local newspaper, and get a radio interview too – all in the same time scale. When your prospective clients see or hear about you on a regular basis, they are more likely to get in touch. There are free ways to get publicity in the papers, magazines, radio and the like, and I'll be talking more about that in Chapter 12.

Promotional material

As a coach or solopreneur, promotional material is one thing you may want to have with you when you go and meet people, attend networking events or in other situations. This can range from business cards, postcards, flyers, expensive glossy postcards, to full colour brochures. I talked about the dos and don'ts of business cards in Chapter 3, step 2, so it may be a good time to refresh your memory.

You could spend a fortune getting professional materials printed, so make sure you get it right. For some solopreneurs, this will be important, for example if you are a therapist, where you may choose to print a price list and information for clients, but for others you would be wise to heed my warnings in this area.

In the early days of my business, I had some promotional material designed and thousands of flyers printed – some of which are still in my cupboard. Although they look lovely, glossy and are professionally printed, they are no longer current. You may find that over time your message and possibly your contact details will change, so take care over the amount of time and money you invest in any such materials. You may find that postcards work better instead and you can buy these in smaller quantities and change your message regularly or even print flyers yourself (as long as you can ensure a quality finish). As I mentioned earlier, with any promotional material, remember it must focus on the client, their problems and how you can solve them, rather than being about you. Benefits, benefits, benefits!

The main time that you will need promotional material is if you are exhibiting at events. This may be your village show, festival, or business event. By now, your message should be clear, you should know the benefits of what you do and who you work with – and if you don't, go back and do some of the exercises before you do any of this!

Having a plan

As you can see, there are a huge number of ways to market your business. The objectives of any marketing activities are to raise your profile and to attract more prospective and actual clients to your business. Therefore, you need a plan. Your marketing plan will set out the objectives for your marketing and the actions you are going to take to reach these objectives. If you implemented every strategy I mentioned, you would struggle to get results. It is all about choosing the strategies that will work for:

- Your business and how you will reach your clients
- What you enjoy doing
- What is going to get you results

Marketing itself will not guarantee you sales, but it will put you in the right place to meet your prospective clients. Also, remember that marketing doesn't stop when you get new clients as this is just the first part of the marketing journey, and you will continue to build long-term and profitable relationships with your clients.

When I interviewed Duncan Brodie for *The Secrets of Successful Coaches*, one of the things he suggested to me is to choose 3 marketing strategies and to do these well, something I mentioned at the beginning of this chapter. For example, if you are in the early stages of your business, you are likely to be filling your funnel with potential prospects and become known, and you may choose to market your business through social media, face-to-face networking and building your list via your website. If your business is more established, your strategy may include speaking and writing to position yourself as an expert, which I will be covering in more detail later. Just remember that your plan needs to be reviewed and tweaked regularly. Assess what works and what doesn't work and what you need to do differently, ensuring that it links into your business mission, objectives and strategy.

One final point when it comes to your marketing plan – set yourself a budget. This may sound a bit alien to some people, because when you set up a business as a solopreneur it is easy to do this without huge overheads, but I would advise you to have a budget. It allows you to make decisions on your marketing based on your budget and how much you have to spend, and keeps you on track from wasting your money on things that don't work.

So go on now, sculpt your plan.

Your plan

What three marketing strategies are you going to implement in your business right now?

1.

2.

3.

How are you going to measure their success?

What needs to happen for these to happen?

What is the first step you are going to take and by when?

Moving onto step 7

In this chapter, I have talked about traditional marketing strategies, but sometimes these are not enough to stand out. Once you have developed your pipeline and have a good list of prospective clients, have some great connections and good relationships, it is time to learn how to set off, stand out and shine. This is what I will be covering in the coming chapters.

Chapter 8
Step 7: Set off, stand out and shine

'Why fit in when you were born to stand out.'
– Dr Seuss

If you have big dreams for your business and are ready to take massive and amazing action, these following chapters are for you. I'll say again though, you must have the building blocks in place, which is why I have shared the entire SUCCESS system with you in this book. If you start with the last 'S', you will be writing a book without understanding the needs of your ideal client, you will be standing on stage without a clear message, and you will be getting PR which isn't right for the growth of your business.

Earlier in this book, I introduced you to the *Pyramid of power and profit* and these chapters aim to help you to go from generalist or specialist to expert. It will help you to become an authority, and be able to communicate this expertise.

Why you need to stand out

Now I know that not everyone reading this book will want to stand out in their business. You may want to keep your business low key, you may not feel you have the confidence to stand out, or you might want to create a small business. This is OK. However, if you want to be successful – whatever this means to you – you will probably need to stand out, even just a little bit. If you think about the statistics I shared with you at the beginning, the 80/20 rule: for many industries, 20% of business owners get 80% of the clients or 80% of the profits, so doesn't it make sense to be one of those 20%?

To be perfectly frank, these days it is not enough to be a bog-standard coach, consultant, therapist, etc. As I mentioned in the introduction, if you are the world's best kept secret, no one will know that you exist, you will struggle to get clients, and you will struggle to fulfil your passion and share your gifts with the world. Alternatively, you may just find you have an expensive hobby and if you are investing money in your development and your business, doesn't it make sense to get clients and get results? If you don't, you'll probably land up going back to your day job or have to find another way to supplement your income.

I also ask you this: Do you want to be the same as everyone else in your industry, or do you want to be different? I certainly believe in modelling, but I also believe that you should choose wisely *who* you model. Think about people in your profession who you look up to or who are your role models. What do they do that gives them the edge or makes them different?

Another caveat for you. You can stand out as much as you like. You don't have to write a book, stand on stage, get in the press, but you can if you want to. I believe it is about doing it your way, being authentic and living your passion. Shaping your vision is the first step of the 7 step system, and when you have this in place, knowing your passion and your 'big why', it does make this last part so much easier.

When I set out in business, I never set out to stand out from the crowd. I started in business as a result of a passion to help people who were in the same position as me. When I found my first coach, I was stuck in a job that I hated and she helped me to find something that I loved to do. However, I quickly realised that if I did just this, I wouldn't be able to make it in business and this led to me modelling top coaches. Through them, I discovered their strategies and developed the 7 steps in this book. I knew that to achieve the success I wanted to achieve, it wouldn't be enough to sit back and let things happen.

I'm not the most extrovert person in the world, although I've grown hugely in confidence over the last six years. The reason I am telling you this is that you don't have to be an extrovert to stand out. You can look at some people in your industry and think you have to be like them, but you don't – it is about being your own authentic you and being happy with it.

This doesn't mean that I don't stretch myself. My goal of getting my message out to people is bigger than me and I do this by writing, standing on stage, and getting PR. I know that these are some of the ways I can achieve what I want to do, and make a difference in this world. I want to be able to help people like you to take those next steps and enable you reach your full potential, thus helping more people to live a more enjoyable and fulfilled life.

The most successful solopreneurs stand out. They do the things that make them unique, different, or attract attention. They don't sit behind their computers and expect things to happen. It may be their niche that makes them stand out, for example, Suzy Greaves markets herself as the Big Leap Coach rather than a Career Coach. This enables her to put a different slant on what she does, and she has published 2 books, which gives her that expert status. It may be that you niche narrow and deep like my friend Helen McCusker whose business is providing PR for book writers and, is therefore, known as the go-to-person for authors. It may be that you are like Roberta Jerram who speaks on stage and inspires business women. It may be that you are like Allison Marlowe, who apart from being a Womanpreneur's Business Mentor, also runs Global Winning Women – networking groups and business awards for women across the UK.

Standing out will allow you to work every day and do what you love, get more clients, help people to live a better life, reach your financial goals, and get results, outcomes and amazing transformations with your clients. Alternatively, perhaps you want to leave a legacy?

How to stand out

There are various ways in which you can stand out in your business. Each of us is unique within our business and you may find that you stand out due to your Unique Selling Proposition (USP). Your USP is what makes your business different in terms of the benefits you give to your clients. What do people think of when they think about you and your business? How do you position yourself? What is your point of difference that makes you stand out?

One of the things that makes me different from other business mentors is the type of people I help (coaches and solopreneurs) and the fact that I have modelled those people who also stand out in their business, which has been one of the secrets to my success. This enables me to share this knowledge and expertise with my clients and enable them to get quick and outstanding results.

You may find that it is your Personality Selling Point (PSP) that makes you different. If you are a solopreneur, what makes you unique in your business is *you*. This may be the reason why people buy you, your services and why they are attracted to working with you.

Part of your PSP, but equally important by itself,

is your own personal story. Your story will often be what has driven you to be who you are or do what you do. Be clear on your story and why it is important. I'll often suggest to my clients to dig deep and think about the 3 things that have had an impact on why they have developed their business, and what has influenced their journey. I'm always amazed by what they tell me.

Another thing that may make you stand out is your expertise. The closer you are to being an expert rather than a generalist or a specialist, the easier it will be for you to attract clients. People will know what you do and you'll become the go-to-person in this area. Many people I know resist this simple concept as they believe that in doing so they are limiting their market, but I believe that in not doing so, they are impeding their success. You've got to do the thing you love to do and that you're good at.

A great way to demonstrate your expertise is by having your own personal signature system. Your system is a process that you work through with your clients, just like the acronym, SUCCESS, which I have shared with you in this book.

When I discovered I had a system, it transformed my business. It enabled me to put together everything I do with my clients into a toolkit of resources and, of course, it enabled me to develop this book in a step-by-step way.

When you are thinking about creating your system, think about the types of activities you do with your clients, the problems you solve, the things you cover time and time again, the transformations you create and then develop your own system. This is another reason why having a clear idea of what you do is so important!

You could use an acronym, or you could choose a model such as the 5 Cs, which my good friend, Carolyn

Barber uses in her business. Having a system makes things easy. No client is the same and you may adapt your system or work with them on part of the system that they need, but it is a good way of getting results and developing an excellent reputation. You can share the results and solutions you get through your system so people know where you are going.

Your signature system

Think about your system – what do you do that works well with your clients?

What are the things you cover repeatedly?

What results do you get?

How can you develop and manage your toolkit?

What needs to happen to develop your system?

Your brand is also important and often your brand (what you show up for) will make someone choose you over someone else or vice versa. This is ultimately made up of everything above and simply being you. You are what people will buy into, so learn how to differentiate yourself from other people in your profession.

One of the concepts I learnt from Lucy Whittington is to have a fame name, just like The Naked Chef or Mary Queen of Shops, which helps people to remember what you do.

Helping you to SHINE

As Dr Seuss said, 'Why fit in when you were born to stand out.' To stand out, you need to learn how to:

Stand up and be counted
Have a passion
Ignite your inner spark
Now get noticed
Elevate your expertise

Stand up and be counted

When you make the decision to stand up and stand out, life will be different. You will naturally attract publicity, and people who understand what you do will want to work with you. If you seriously think about your achievements, your successes, your expertise, you will find it easy to work out how you can stand out from everyone else.

Have a passion

Going back to my 7 Step SUCCESS System, remember Step 1 – Shape your vision? Your vision is made up of various elements but most importantly, your purpose, your passion and 'big why'. When you know your 'big why' it will enable you to shine and propel you to take action. It will force you to share your bigger mission through your passion for helping your clients. It will give you the momentum to do the things that scare you; you will take action and make big things happen. Having that passion will make business so much easier as it will make you do the things that you're unsure about right now.

Ignite your inner spark

Shine is about standing up and being counted. It is about having a vision and igniting your inner spark. This is the passion, excitement and energy you have when you are reaching your true potential. It is about your mindset, something I've shared with you already in this book. Your mindset can make or break your business success. Your mindset is about your attitudes, approaches, beliefs and confidence you have towards achieving what you want.

When was the last time you ignited your inner spark?

How can you keep up your energy levels and play full out?

It is easy to belittle yourself, focus on the negatives and stop yourself achieving your full potential. You may find that you are limited by your mind, but you can always do more than you think you can do.

What will it cost if you fail to eliminate what holds you back?

You just need to make the decision to do it and not be wavering. This reminds me of the metaphor of firewalking where you can't hesitate – you just have to raise your energy, get your focus and then make the decision to do it.

Now get noticed

Like any goal you want to attain, you need to:

1. Know where you are
2. Know where you are going
3. Create a plan
4. Follow the plan
5. Expect the best

When you want to be noticed, this will mean different things. You might want to tell people what you are doing, get into the press, get other publicity, attract more clients, or something else.

If you think about a financial goal, you need to know what your bank balance is, and know what you want to be earning or your ideal profit. You then may need a plan to create options to spend less or earn more, to put prices up or to acquire more clients, and then you have to pursue your plan by making sure your mindset is in the right place. At all times you must expect the best rather than sabotaging your success.

Therefore, become noticed, dream big, and make it happen.

Elevate your expertise

The most successful solopreneurs have a support team. This will include coaches and mentors, who share success strategies, motivate them, inspire them and make them accountable to taking action. They will help them to elevate their expertise and be masters at what they do and how they leverage their knowledge.

There are three steps to mastery:

1. Modelling – watch how others do what they do
2. Immersion – immerse yourself into the experience
3. Repetition – by repeating the success strategies rather than giving up

You need to find that way in which you elevate your expertise, which I will be covering in the coming chapters. You need to find a way to leverage your success, such as getting great publicity, writing a book or speaking on stage.

So what stops you?

Before you consider tangible strategies to stand out, you need to focus on the things that might stop you.

You might think that you are not good enough or that you don't have enough experience. There are too many solopreneurs who want to become more experienced, knowledgeable, and get another qualification before they take further action. NO! Just get on with it! If this applies to you, please re-read the chapters Cultivate your confidence and Cut the crap. Learn how to get out of your own way and achieve the success you really desire. When you know what you really want and have a compelling reason for doing it, nothing will stop you from achieving the success you desire.

Perhaps you just want clients to find you and this reminds me of a conversation I had with a client. She told me that she didn't want to sell and she wanted to be known as the go-to-person in her area of expertise and for people to find her. I'm sorry, but in today's competitive marketplace, this isn't going to happen overnight. Even if you do reach the status of people knowing about you and contacting you, you will still need to sell the benefits of what you do (more about that in the next chapter).

You just need to go forth, stand out, and take action. In the next chapter, we will take a look at strategies to do this.

Remember you can get access to more resources, information and tips at www.HowToStandOut.co.uk. So register now to stand out and shine even more brightly.

Chapter 9
Stand out by selling

'A clear vision, backed by definite plans,
gives you a tremendous feeling of
confidence and personal power.'
– *Brian Tracy*

If you are a solopreneur wanting to create a successful business, I'm sorry to tell you this, but you have to sell. Selling seems to be a swear word to many new coaches and solopreneurs but this is a fear you will have to overcome fast. If you don't sell your services, you won't have a business! It's no good being the best in your profession if no one wants to invest in what you do.

To stand out by selling does not mean forcing a service or product on someone who doesn't want it; it is about giving people what they want. I believe that successful selling for solopreneurs is about doing so in an authentic and heartfelt way. If you think about it, your prospective clients have contacted you because they recognise that you have the solution to their problems, so you would do them a disservice if you didn't tell them how you can help them.

For those of you who remain unconvinced, would it help if you reframed the word 'selling'? Is it about recommending products and services that work? Or, is it about inviting prospective clients to buy the service that you are offering? If you are convinced and are happy to sell, I'm sure you're already doing this well!

From my experience of working with coaches, one of the first things that many of them struggle with is asking for money. Hey, I was one of these people six years ago! For many of them, they spend their time whilst training, providing their coaching services for free (pro bono) in exchange for a testimonial and feedback for their qualification. Then, when it comes to asking for money from a client, they may struggle to do so.

There are many reasons why this may be the case. If this resonates with you, it may be because you don't yet feel experienced and ready to charge for your services. Nevertheless, how will you get experience unless you go out there and do it? Also, think about the knowledge and experience that has led you up to this point and makes you the expert that you already are.

For some of you, you may feel that you can't charge the same amount of money as other people in your profession. If this is the case, I ask you why not? If this is really an issue for you, start charging lower fees and work your way up incrementally so you feel comfortable (although please don't undercharge for a valuable service). Although in saying that, being uncomfortable is certainly a great place to start!

How you feel about selling may also depend on your client. If you are working with a multi-national organisation, you may feel more comfortable about charging higher fees than if you were working with someone who had just lost their job.

You do need to value your knowledge, your experience and your expertise. What I have found is that the clients I have who are less able to afford my fees are those who put more effort into achieving what they want to accomplish. Often just making a huge investment is motivation enough for someone to be committed to achieving outstanding results.

When you offer your service for free or at low cost, people are less likely to value the service and will put less effort into achieving their goal, as there won't be the pressure behind it. In addition, I believe that it negates your profession if you don't charge what you are worth.

Think about it this way. Would you value someone's advice more if they provided it for free or if you paid good money for it?

How would you feel if you did what you did free of charge or at low cost and you couldn't actually sustain your business or make any money from it?

Getting your pricing right

Getting your pricing right is incredibly important. Earlier in the book, I talked about having different products and programmes because not every prospective one-to-one client is going to pay you hundreds or thousands of pounds. When you have multiple products and programmes, it makes it easier to satisfy the needs of your clients (as long as you give them what they want and don't confuse them with the options!).

How do you get it right? Firstly, you have to get out of your own way. It is easy to worry that you are overpricing (or even under pricing yourself) and especially if it is the former, you have to trust that people will pay for what you are offering. I hope you did your market research first! As I mentioned earlier, it is important to value and recognise your expertise. If you doubt yourself, this may well come across to your clients.

Remember that you are an expert and when you present yourself in this way, people are likely to see your value. Give your clients value for their investment and share with them the benefits of working with you and achieving what they want. Do not devalue yourself, lower your prices, or give things away free of charge. Learn how to focus on prosperity. When your clients see you as an expert, they will come back for more and recommend you to others.

One tip is to package up what you do. I never offer a one-off coaching or mentoring session to a client and, although this may be different depending upon your profession, how could you package up what you do or add additional value?

- If you are a coach, could you provide a package of 6 or 8 coaching sessions?
- If you offer a VIP day, could you add follow-up mentoring calls?
- If you offer training to an organisation, could you add follow-up coaching or support, or even a programme of training sessions?
- If you are a virtual assistant, could you offer a monthly package comprising of a certain number of hours of work with you?
- If you are a therapist, could you offer a package for a course of 4 treatments?
- If you are a marketer or web designer, could you offer a monthly retainer?
- How else can you add value to your programmes and packages?

Consider this – are people going to get even better results when you have the time to facilitate the change? Would this not be an even better result for you and your client?

One further thought for you to consider – would you prefer working with 10 clients paying you £500 a programme or 5 clients paying you £1000 a programme? When you value yourself and you charge what you are worth, this allows you the time and the money to invest in yourself and give an even better service to your clients.

At this stage you may be thinking, 'This is all well and good, but how do I actually get these prospective clients in the first place?'

Well every profession is different. I remember when I interviewed Michael Neill for *The Secrets of Successful Coaches*, he told me that all you need to do to get a client is to have a conversation. How can you have more conversations in your business?

The 3 step process to attract clients

One of the things I do most successfully to attract new clients is to follow this 3 step process. This is certainly relevant for coaches and consultants who are providing a high quality (and high value) solution for their clients. I'm sure all of you will be able to take what you need from this process and apply these strategies to your business.

Before I share the process with you, I want to add a caveat. It is going to be more difficult to do this if you have not taken the other steps in the book, so if you've rushed forward, make sure you go back and do these first:

- You've got to know your passions and your talents
- You've got to find a way of telling your prospective clients that you exist
- You've got to be able to give your clients a service that they want
- You've got to do something a little different to stand out from the crowd
- You need to know the transformations your clients get from working with you
- You've got to give prospective clients an opportunity to speak with you

- You've got to be comfortable in selling yourself and your services or at least be willing to learn

Have you got these in place? Let me share with you the 3 steps:

3 steps to get more clients

1. Invite people to have a conversation with you
2. Have the conversation
3. Give them what they want

Let's go through these in more detail:

1. Invite people to have a conversation with you

Every month I offer my prospective clients the opportunity to have a 20-minute success discovery session with me, which is a way in which they can talk to me for free. You may be asking yourself, 'Why? Hasn't Karen said we must value our knowledge and expertise?'

A discovery session is not a coaching session, nor is it a mentoring session, It is a way of exploring what my prospective clients want, what they would like to be different and how I can help them to achieve this objective. A discovery session ascertains what the problem is, not how to solve it. I will usually send out a questionnaire to the individual prior to the session to find out more about them and to qualify them as a suitable prospective client.

There are various ways in which you can invite this conversation. You could offer it through your newsletter list, on social media, when you are at a networking event, when you are a speaker at an event, or when you initially speak with a prospective client. If you work with organisations, you are automatically likely to have this type of conversation when you speak with the decision maker to take a proposal forward for consideration.

2. Have the conversation

Assume that you have invited someone to have a conversation with you and now's the time for the chat. What are the strategies that work?

You could have a script, but you might find this a bit clunky. Better still, you could have some powerful questions that work.

For those of you who are coaches, you will be using your coaching skills – listening, questioning and exploring. You are in a great position to put your skills to the test. You will be giving the prospective client the time and space to think, dream and explore, something they may never have done before. You will be finding out their wants, needs, goals and aspirations. You will be exploring what they have done before, what has worked, and what didn't get them results.

Whether it is a corporate client or an individual, these are some of the aspects you may consider when having this initial conversation:

Introduce the discovery session so they know what to expect during the time in which you are talking with them.

Tell your client something about you that is relevant to their situation. Your story, knowledge and expertise are important – so be clear about what you want to say.

Find out where they are right now. Ask them

questions about their career, business, health, lifestyle, organisation, or whatever is appropriate. For example:

- What was it that inspired/motivated you to speak with me?
- If anything could happen as a result of this conversation, what would it be?
- What inspired you to ...?
- What is your big dream/aim/objective of ...?
- Why is this important?
- Where are you right now with ...?

Then if it is relevant, find out what is stopping them right now. For example:

- What action have you taken so far?
- What would happen if you did nothing right now?
- What is important about the support you receive from someone?

Get them to see the possibilities of what they could achieve with support (think benefits not features). Then as part of this conversation, move onto step 3.

3.   Give them what they want

If you can help the person with their problem, i.e. you are the expert they seek, what can you offer them?

Tell them about the product or service that will solve their problem or meet their need.   Share with them the transformations and benefits that it will give them or their organisation. Be confident and congruent when you present your price and package.

Just remember it is about helping people to buy what they want rather than selling something they don't need.

Managing objections

The 3 step process might look easy, but you may find it more difficult in practice. Remember that your product or service is not going to be right for everyone and the way you present it is important. It is likely that your prospective clients will have objections to what you are offering them, so part of the process is being able to recognise and overcome their doubts.

Objections are those things that stop a prospective client from buying from you. That's not to say that you have to force them into buying from you; it's about finding an authentic way to present your offer and being able to counter the objections they may be sharing with you.

The best way to manage objections is to recognise and respond to them before they are raised, but in saying that, you need to understand the types of objections that your clients may raise. Typical objections in service-based industries relate to:

- Price, cost, value – if the price is perceived high against the value, the prospective client may be worried about whether or how they will recoup this investment, or whether they will get value from working with you. They may also compare it against other items of a similar cost
- Time – the prospective client may feel that they are not ready to take action, that they don't have enough time to do it justice, or that they need it

sooner or later than you propose delivering the solution
- Credibility – the prospective client may not yet trust that you can deliver the solution or that it will work for them
- Knowledge – the prospective client may believe they have enough knowledge to do it by themselves or perhaps have insufficient knowledge to know whether you are offering them the right solution

Price is the most common objection faced by solopreneurs, especially when it comes to a perceived high cost/high value solution. Overcoming objections enables people to feel happy with what you are offering them and trust that you can deliver what they want for the right price, in the timescales available. One of the other reasons for offering a discovery session or a complimentary meeting in a corporate environment is so that both parties can explore whether it would suit them to work together.

Overcoming these objections is going to be different for each of you, but firstly you need to have a 100% belief in what you do, your product or service, and the results you provide your clients. Put yourself in your customer's shoes and consider the types of things that may stop them making the buying decision. Also, if people are reluctant to say yes to you, ask them what is stopping them from working with you. This allows you to address these issues there and then by talking them through with the individual.

You may wish to share personal stories, case studies (respecting confidentiality), results that other clients have achieved by working with you and you may also offer to put them in touch with previous or current clients. You may want to (nicely) point out what will happen if they don't take action or do something about what is holding them back. You may also wish to offer fast action bonuses when someone commits to working with you immediately. Importantly, know the benefits and transformations that clients get from working with you and share them with your prospective clients. If they don't say yes straight away, make sure you agree a time to follow up in the next few days.

Why and how people buy

There are two main reasons why people buy – one is to avoid pain and the other is to create more pleasure – so you need to tell people the benefits of working with you and how they can create those benefits. A great way to do this is to reflect back their language to them and recognise their motivators.

For example, if you are a therapist, some people will want a massage to reduce stress (so avoiding pain) and others will want time to relax (to create pleasure). If you are a relationship coach, some people may want to stop being single and others will want to find a loving partner. In an organisation, some HR managers will want to reduce sickness levels and others may want to promote positive well-being.

When someone recommends a prospective client or they have indicated an interest in working with you, they are more likely to buy your products or services. That is not to say that other people won't commit to working with you. Just notice when they are interested in what you have to say. If they start asking you about your prices, ask you questions about the number of sessions, make positive noises or ask you when the programme can start, they are showing an interest in working with you. My top tip is when you tell them the price and the value of the programme, allow them time to consider your offer rather than jump in with reasons why they should work with you or start justifying your fees!

People generally buy on emotion and then justify with logic, so I'm sure you can see how, by having a conversation, you can tap into the reasons why they need to make the changes they wish to make.

So what do you need to do to have more sales conversations?

Understand the science of persuasion

One of the books that turned my business around was *The Psychology of Persuasion* by Robert Cialdini. He talks about the 6 principles of persuasion, which is an essential book to read if you want to understand how you can persuade people in business, either through your website, marketing copy, or through selling. Here is a short summary of the 6 principles:

Principles of persuasion

Liking – people want to do business with people they can relate to. A great way to do this through your marketing is via video and social media and, of course, a telephone or face-to-face meeting can accelerate this liking.

Authority – people want to know about you and your credentials, experience and knowledge. Through your marketing, you can do this by telling people about your story, your website, professional accreditations, and through a conversation, you can tell them about your experience and expertise.

Scarcity – if something is limited or scarce, people are likely to take more rapid action. This includes limited time offers or bonuses for a defined period, which could be considered when having a conversation or meeting someone.

Consistency/commitment – when you encourage someone to commit to something, they are more likely to go through with this commitment. This can include committing to an appointment or signing up to a programme.

Reciprocity – this is best seen when you offer a freebie on your website in return for someone's email address. Although in a conversation, someone may be inclined to suggest you to a friend or colleague even if you are not the right person for them.

Social proof – in business, testimonials and recommendations are the most common ways of showing social proof. You may also share case studies and stories to demonstrate your worth.

Like all of the information in this book, approach these principles with authenticity and care, and do not exert influence, manipulate or coerce – but you know that anyway!

Knowing how to sell and understanding the principles of persuasion are tools that you require in order to stand out in your business. Let's take these aspects a stage further. Now it is time to discover how you can stand out on stage!

Chapter 10
Stand out on stage

'Many of life's failures are people who did not realize how close they were to success when they gave up.'
– *Thomas A. Edison*

I believe that if you want to be one of the crowd, you will be someone who attends networking meetings. If you want to stand out, you will be either the person running the networking group or the person standing on stage. When I talk about standing on stage, this may not literally mean standing on a stage (although it might), but could be presenting a talk at a networking group, conference, or running your own event.

The thought of standing on stage might scare you and if it does, that's fine. Apparently, public speaking is one of the main fears faced by humans. Of course, you have a choice as to whether you want to overcome this and do something about your fear to get your message out there, or whether you find another way to share your expertise.

If you are truly committed to standing out in your business, being a speaker is very important. So why is this? In my view, there are various reasons.

Firstly, you get to share your message with more people, some of whom may not have had access to your knowledge until you made that decision to speak. If you think about it, are you going to touch more lives if you talk one-to-one or one-to-many? In taking that leap, you have the ability to change many people's lives for the better. Is that not a good enough reason in itself?

Secondly, the more you speak, the more confident you will feel. Honestly! Yes, you will always learn from what has gone well and how you can improve. Therefore, what is the worst (and the best) that could happen?

Thirdly, when you stand on stage you gain greater credibility (as long as you do a good job!) and people will see you as an expert in your field.

Lastly, you have the opportunity to make more sales and generate more money in your business. As long as you are giving your prospective clients what they want, are clear about what you offer, and get this message across, this is a great benefit of standing on stage.

Getting speaking gigs

You may feel that you would be happy standing on stage and speaking, but you don't know where to start with finding speaking engagements. Finding a safe, secure environment, like your local networking groups who want speakers like you, is a great place to start. You could contact your local speakers' club, such as Toastmasters (www.toastmasters.org), where you will find a safe and secure environment in which to gain confidence in speaking.

In my experience, the best speaking engagements are those where you can find your ideal clients, so if you are struggling to arrange talks, ask your contacts, put a post or two on your social media platforms, or create your own opportunities through putting on your own event. When you put the message out there that you want to do more speaking (think about the Law of Attraction), you are likely to get more opportunities coming your way.

You might be thinking about how much to charge, what you would speak about and how you can make money from speaking etc. So let me address some of these aspects.

Most local networking groups will not pay you to speak. They may pay your expenses, but most have no budget to pay you a fee. Like many situations, it's about finding a win-win solution as you will be giving up your time and energy for these talks. In these situations, it is worth finding out whether you can promote your services from the stage. Speaking opportunities may not result in immediate income (of course, there is a likelihood it will); as with many of the strategies in the next few chapters, they may lead to acquiring more clients as you learn how to leverage your success. If you are speaking at conferences, large events or providing a keynote, it is possible to command a fee for speaking.

In terms of choosing a topic to speak about, remember earlier, I talked about creating a signature system? Why not share one of the steps in your system? If you have a large agenda with multiple things to talk about, it is going to confuse the audience, but if you have a key message (keeping it simple), it makes more sense to you and your audience. I have a one-page PDF Speaker Profile that I send to organisers when I am asked (or offer) to speak to groups, which makes it easier for me and the person sourcing a speaker. During the talk, I will share my system, talk about the part that is relevant to the audience, and then tell people how they can get the whole system and work with me (and of course, get a copy of my books).

Speaking hints and tips

Like in any new situation, you have just a few seconds to make a great first impression. Therefore, I would like to share with you some tips that have worked well for me.

Know your outcomes:

Before you create and write your presentation, start with the end in mind and know the outcome that you want to create. If you have the opportunity to sell from the stage, your outcome may be that they buy your product or service, and if this is the case, work back from this offer when you put together your talk.

If you are sharing great information, what do you want the audience to do, say or feel at the end of your talk? Obviously, you need to pitch your talk at the appropriate level for your audience and their knowledge of your subject. Know your message and what you want people to do after they hear your talk.

Prepare your presentation:

Everyone is different when it comes to preparing a presentation. Don't create death by PowerPoint, have too much or too little information to share, or have the wrong information for the wrong audience. Therefore, preparation is key.

Even if you have the best presentation in the world, be mindful that you will have many people in the room with different perceptions and ways of looking at things. They are giving up their time to listen and learn from you and you need to be able to give each and every one of them exactly what they want. No pressure then!

The most important thing is being able to engage the audience from the start, so let me share with you a system that works. The 4MAT system is a great way to structure the first couple of minutes of your presentation and make the right first impression. The 4MAT system is made up of 4 areas that when you address each of them in your introduction and in order, (when done well), it will immediately engage your audience:

4MAT System

WHY?
Why are people interested in your talk?
Why should they be there?
Give them some reasons for listening to you and why you are an expert

NB Ask your audience some questions. ('Yes sets' are a great tool to do this, when you ask 3 questions that your audience are likely to answer with the word yes)

WHAT?
What are you going to talk about?
Give them the bigger picture about your talk
Tell them what is included
NB Tell them what you are going to tell them, and share with them 3 key points that they will learn

HOW?
How does your talk affect them?
How can they use the information after the session?
Tell them the practicalities of what you are going to share
NB Tell them how your presentation will work, for example, when you are accepting questions, whether it is interactive, etc.

WHAT IF?
Remind them of the key messages that you will be sharing
Link your presentation to the benefits of listening to you
Tell people how they will feel if they have implemented what you are going to tell them
NB This is a great time to pre-frame that you will be telling them later on how they can find out more about you and how they can work with you further

Practise, practise, practise

Once you have the 4MAT system nailed and you have the outline for your presentation, practice is essential. You may choose to practise in your head, out loud, in front of a mirror or with friends. Either way, just remember to practise. You don't want to be reading from slides or your notes (although a crib sheet is OK), so knowing your stuff is essential to enhance your credibility.

Managing your nerves

Even the most seasoned presenters have nerves when they are standing up in front of people. To be honest, if you don't have a few nerves when speaking in front of a group of people, I would be surprised. A few nerves will keep you on your toes and get you focused. There are many strategies that you can employ to overcome nerves, but I would suggest that if this is the case, get some presentations skills training or support to improve your abilities and overcome whatever is holding you back.

If you are a little nervous, anchoring is a great

technique to use. If you haven't come across anchoring before, let me give you an example. Anchoring is what occurs naturally when you hear a song that reminds you of a holiday or you smell something like coffee, which elicits a positive or negative response. With anchoring, you can create a resourceful state, such as confidence which you can access when you need it, for example, as you are getting ready to do your talk. To anchor this state, start by remembering a time when you were confident (it need not be when you were speaking, but it could be). When you are fully immersed into the experience and remember what you saw, heard and felt, anchor the feeling by touching part of your body, such as your forefinger and thumb. Practise the anchoring and reinforce it. Then when you need it, you can fire it off to give you that boost of confidence.

Another good way to prepare for your talk is to model other people who do great presentations. What do they do that makes them outstanding? What are their preparation strategies? How can you model them?

Just remember to unleash your passion, be focused, raise your energy and go for it!

Selling from stage

If you have read the previous chapter, you will already know my views on selling. I would like to introduce a few more tips about selling from stage.

Selling from stage strategies

1. Make sure you have permission to sell from the stage
2. Have a product or service that is right for your

audience, for example, selling a high value one-to-one programme may not be appropriate but a lower value item could work very well.

3. When you put your programme together, start from your offer and then work out your content. Remember to pre-frame the fact that you will be making an offer when you start your presentation.

4. Be clear on your offer and the benefits to your audience.

5. You may wish to consider fast action bonuses that are only available when people purchase the programme on the day of your presentation.

6. Don't answer questions about your offer in front of the audience. Give people the chance to come to you after the talk and ask you questions privately, as you don't want one person's opinion to cloud the minds of the other audience members.

7. Having the option to create the buying opportunity straight after the talk or in a break before other distractions is a good position to be in.

Follow up

The most important thing to remember when you are speaking in front of a ready-made crowd is to make sure you acquire the contact details of the individuals in your audience. If you are not able to sell from stage, offer a free report, a free discovery session, do a prize draw, or something else. Then remember to follow up!

Getting help to stand out on stage

If you know that appearing on stage will help you to

become noticed, seek some help to get yourself out there. Therefore, if you have decided that you are ready to stand out on stage, what is the first action step that you are going to take?

Don't forget that you can access more resources and information at www.HowToStandOut.co.uk and feel free to ask my advice to help you to stand out successfully on stage.

Chapter 11
Stand out on the page

'Success is the sum of small efforts, repeated day in and day out.' – Robert Collier

Do you remember I mentioned the *Pyramid of power and profit* earlier in this book? The best way in which you can be an 'expert' is by writing a book. Suffice to say that you are unlikely to make millions or save for your retirement by getting published. According to statistics, the average book in America sells about 500 copies (Publishers Weekly, July 17, 2006). So why do it?

It is said that we all have a book within us (and perhaps more), and there are many reasons why people write a book. For solopreneurs it is often about sharing their expertise with a wider audience who may not have been able to access this knowledge before the book was published. It may also be about achieving the status of expert, or for the personal or commercial reason of leveraging their knowledge. It could well be a combination of all of these. Writing a book is a great way to showcase yourself as an expert; it is a great business card when you meet someone for the first time, or as a stepping stone to speaking, positive publicity and achieving greater success.

I love to write and I've been told that I'm good at it. It enables me to share my message with more people than I can do on a one-to-one basis. In addition, I know I have an important message to share, and I can do this by using my favourite medium.

However, unless you have already put pen to paper, or hand to keyboard, you may be wondering where to start when you write a book, so let me share with you some strategies in this chapter.

Start with the end in mind

Do I need to mention the SUCCESS system again? You should know by now that having each of these elements in place is going to elevate your success, and the same goes for writing your book. You know that I go by the premise, start with the end in mind, and nothing is truer when it comes to writing your book. Before you even start to write, you need to have some crucial elements in place.

Know your intention behind writing your book

Why do you want to write your book? Be 100% clear on this reason as the passion or 'big why' for writing your book is what will get you up at 5 a.m. with new ideas, and will spur you on to completing your writing. It is not enough to be really fired up in the beginning because I'm sure you want to finish your book, and perhaps write another as well. Is your intention about your message? How does it fit into your wider business plan, goals and dreams? How can you keep going when you start to run out of steam?

Be clear on your topic

Being clear on your topic may seem obvious but is often overlooked when people come to write a book. They want to share everything they know but forget to structure the book in an easy to follow process – this is where having a system or way of working comes to its own. Start with a message, a topic, a story, or a passion that you want to share with others.

Know your topic

When you are writing your book, you will probably be doing your research, supplementing your knowledge, and sourcing advice and stories from others to be able to write it. Make sure that you are writing about a subject that you know well, one in which you are an expert as this will make it easier for both you and your readers.

Know who will buy your book

Have a clear idea of your target audience – who do you envisage will be reading your book? If you already work with people who want to be healthy, it makes sense to build on your specialism and write a book for the people you work with already. Ask yourself the following questions: 'Why should they buy it?' 'What will they get from reading my book?' 'Do they want it?' If in doubt, ask the people you work with, find out what they want and then go ahead and provide it.

Be clear about your audience just like I did in step 5: Are your readers male or female? What age are they? What do they do for a living? What is their background? What are their hopes, dreams and desires?

You will want to be sure that your market is big enough to make an impact but small enough to be targeted to their needs and not too general.

Check out the competition

Do your market research before you start writing your book. Who has written similar books already? What else has already been written in this area? What makes your book different?

You may wish to buy some of the other books that have been written about your topic and find out what other people have to say, and what makes your book unique. If no one has written about your topic before, what is the reason behind this?

Get planning

At this stage, you are probably ready to write. You know you have a topic that you are passionate about, that people will read, that you are very knowledgeable about, and you know that no one does it exactly the way you do. So where do you start? Do you just write and hope it will happen? My advice is to get planning first. You don't want to get a few thousand words in and then need to start again, do you?

Before you start to write, start to plan what you want to say. Gather all the information you have on your topic, whether these are interviews, your own notes, PowerPoint presentations, useful information you have learnt from others, books, videos, audios and more. Then you can start to put this information together. I find it easier to start with a big brainstorm or mind map.

When I wrote my first book, *The Secrets of Successful Coaches*, I took pages of flipchart paper and different coloured post-it notes and literally planned my chapters in this way. I worked out my topics, sub-topics and put them into a logical order. I worked out what I had to say and how it all fitted together. This was a slightly different process to how I put together *How To Stand Out In Your Business,* as I had interviewed 11 successful coaches and I was wading through the advice, titbits and quotes that they had shared with me. I needed to find an easy way to present this in a logical and cohesive order. There was a lot of planning and re-planning I can tell you! Eventually, I came up with 10 key messages that I wanted to share which made up the main chapters of the book.

When I wrote this book, I started with pages of mind maps. Don't forget, I already had my system so I knew how I wanted to sequence the book, and the mind maps focused on each step of the system and what I wanted to share with you, my reader. I had the information in many formats as I regularly share these steps with my clients. I have a toolkit of information and I had a vision behind what I wanted to create. If you have never done a mind map before, this is how I did it. I started with the chapter heading in the middle of the page, and then literally mapped out the sub-sections; these sub-sections led to more notes about what I wanted to include in each chapter. Therefore, you need a big piece of paper!

On the subject of planning, you will find that your mind map or whatever system you use for planning will move on as you write your book. I will admit that these last few chapters morphed as I started writing and became individual chapters in their own right rather than the last step as originally planned. This mainly came from developing the Star Biz conference, my very first multi-speaker business conference, where these topics will take centre stage, and by talking to my clients and finding out about the strategies they wanted to learn about.

However you do this planning stage, I believe it is the most important part of the process. It makes it much easier to write a chapter when you have a logical structure of what you want to share, and it saves on duplication, endless editing and frustration when the words don't flow and the ... 'Oh, you know what I mean!' By the time you reach this stage you should know the number of chapters you will have, the titles and outlines for each chapter, all following a logical order and how they will be organised and sequenced.

Another tip from me – before I write each chapter, I look at my mind map and literally sequence the chapter with a brain dump of everything I want to include, just in case I missed something in my early planning. Then I sequence it, which makes it easy to write and pick it up again at a later stage.

When you are in the planning stage, think about how you are going to write your book. You may decide to do what I do and just type straight into your computer as the words come into your head. If you are more auditory inclined, you may prefer to dictate your book and have someone type it up for you or use a piece of software that will turn your audio into type. You may want to handwrite your book and get someone to type it for you. You may even wish to employ someone who takes your ideas and then writes it for you. Which method will you choose?

Schedule your time

Talking about picking things up at a later stage, I am assuming that you won't be spending all of your time writing. I'm sure you will be fitting it in around client appointments; marketing your business and everything else you need to do to bring in an income and make your time work effectively. It is important to schedule some (quiet) time into your writing. As I write this chapter and finish the first draft of my book, I have scheduled a week 'off' work for this purpose entirely – yes, there has been some downtime, but equally there have been long periods of writing, just as I am doing today.

So set up a work schedule for your writing. Is there a particular time of day when your juices flow more creatively? I am particularly known to have 5 a.m. ideas which get me up and writing in my PJs before others start for the day. It is having a plan and, dare I say, goals that will help you to keep your writing on track. Set yourself blocks of time, no less than 90 minutes to write and then stick to it. What timescale do you have to complete your book? What needs to happen for that to happen?

Just get writing

It may be easy to say, but the next step is to just get writing. As I mentioned above, you could choose to dictate it instead of writing it, or you may find that writing it by hand works better for you. If you are not sure that you are a writer, what evidence have you got to think this? We can all write in our own way and you could get someone to do it for you. You may be like me in that I write as I speak and the advantage of this is that many people have said to me that when they read my books, they can hear me speaking it!

If you think about it, if someone picks up your book, they may start reading from Chapter 1 and you are going to want to grab their attention on this very first page. You're going to want to make it easy to read and in bite-sized chunks, but more about that later. Just write for now.

When I wrote this and my first book, I literally wrote it and then edited it later. If you start editing it as you go, you'll find it more difficult to complete and actually get it done. It may not be perfect, but you will have the bones of what you want to say and you can make it even better and correct the typos later.

Editing your book

To be honest, I have found editing my book one of the hardest parts. You want to make your writing punchy, get the right message across, check for typos and so much more. You will probably want to do an initial edit, where you will read your entire book, check for typos, grammatical errors, and check for sense, readability and flow. Then you will probably edit in more detail, by taking each chapter, making sure it is in manageable chunks and easy to read.

Finally, you start back at the beginning. Write your acknowledgements to thank those who have helped you with your book, your introduction telling people why they need to read your book, get some testimonials, and perhaps (if you haven't done so already) contact your ideal role model to write your foreword for you.

You may find that more editing will happen when you move through the book. When I write my books, I always get other people to read it for me. When I wrote my first book I asked my Dad to read it for me and I had a friend to do the same (my Dad is a stickler for grammar, so this was useful, especially, as I just mentioned, I write like I talk!) As with any piece of writing, when you do it yourself you are very close to the material. You don't see the errors that other people will see; the 'you' that should be 'your', the 'it' that should be an 'if' and those other pesky errors that your spell check doesn't pick up. By the way, if you see one of those blasted mistakes in this book, then they are my gift to you!

I hope that this information helps you to put together your own book because when I wrote *The Secrets of Successful Coaches* I really didn't have a clue and it took me eighteen months to complete it from end to end. I started my interviews with successful coaches in August 2009, which finished with Michael Neill on 27 December 2009. During that time, I started to plan the book and write it. My goal was to have it completed by Easter 2010 (which I admit didn't happen) and there were a few things that stopped me along the way (but more about that in a minute). I didn't know what I needed to do to get my book published, let alone promote it!

One of the things I found out in August 2010 is that I needed a professional copy editor and proofreader. You may chose not to have one, but I found that mine helped me to get consistency across the book and made suggestions about how to improve it further.

What if ...?

I mentioned in the last section that a couple of things slowed me down when I wrote my first book. Some of these were the practicalities of not knowing what to do and another was my mindset. Yes, shocking I know as I teach this stuff to my clients, but valid all the same. I went through a few wobbles ... 'What if no one buys my book?' 'What if it isn't a success?' 'What if it isn't very good?' I'm sure you get the picture. Don't allow the 'what ifs' to get in your way. Just do it and just know that it will be successful. Although I experienced the 'what ifs', writing my first book did literally propel my business success.

Getting published

One of the reasons for this chapter is to help you to learn from some of my mistakes. Although getting published is far down the list of things you need to do, it doesn't mean you need to leave it until last.

The beauty of getting your book published in the

twenty-first century is that there are numerous ways in which you can do it. You can seek a traditional publisher, you can choose an option like partnership publishing or you can publish it yourself. I looked at all of these options the first time round. I contacted traditional publishers, but found that many of their timescales were not the same as mine, and they are much more discerning than they used to be. There are many people like you who want to write a book and traditional publishers don't offer huge advances (unless you are a well-known name) and it is extremely difficult to get a contract, especially if yours is a niche book.

If you decide to go down this route yourself, check out the publishers that produce books of your genre, and how they would like you to approach them – the *Authors and Writer's Year Book* is a good place to start. Each publisher is different; some will accept manuscripts; some will accept only the first five pages and others want just an overview, so check what they want first and make sure you submit what they want. Some won't accept manuscripts anymore as they are literally bombarded with people wanting to get their books published! Some of the questions I have asked you already will stand you in good stead for getting a publisher. One of the traditional publishers was interested in my first book (but it took nine months to get to this stage), and I had decided to go down the partnership publishing route by then. You may also decide to get a literary agent to help you, but this depends on the right option for you.

When I published my first book, I did so in partnership with Matador, and there are other options including Ecademy Press, where you can work with Mindy Gibbins-Klein 'The Book Midwife', who can help you get yourself into print as part of a programme. There are other small publishing companies, all of whom work in partnership with you to help you to publish your book. Yes, there is a fee, but the company takes over some of the more complicated things you may not wish to be involved in, such as getting an ISBN – (International Standard Book Number which is essential if you want to sell your book on Amazon and in book stores), registering with the British Library (in the UK), producing your book cover, design and image, helping you to choose the right sized book, typesetting, printing your book, getting your book on Kindle and other e-readers, and the things that can take a while if you are not an expert. You know what I have to say on this subject – if it's not your thing, get someone else to do it for you!

You could, of course, decide to go down the self-publishing route where you will do some of the hard work yourself (or get someone to do it for you), for example, with an online print-on-demand publisher such as Lulu and CompletelyNovel.

Your first copy!

I will never forget the day I received the first copies of *The Secrets of Successful Coaches.* I had to ask my husband to undo the box and take out a copy just in case I didn't like it! But I loved it. It was one of my proudest and most excited moments.

This is where having a plan comes into its own, or at least it did for me. I already had my book launch party planned, with over 80 attendees ready to celebrate my success, so having my book arrive in time was an important part of the plan!

My experiences of writing a book

I hope that sharing some of my experiences has helped you to start to plan and write your book. I have been candid in my sharing and I know that through learning from my mistakes, this book took me six months from planning to publication rather than the eighteen months that it took for *The Secrets of Successful Coaches.* It does help that my goal is to have this book in my hands when I run the Star Biz conference in November 2012.

Marketing your book

In terms of marketing your book, it is essential that you learn how to leverage your book, and publicise it to achieve sales. However you decide to publish, even if you go through a traditional publisher, you will still need to take action to market your book further. Here are a few ideas and I'll be talking more about leverage later.

Book marketing tips

- Have a party or event to celebrate your book launch
- Tell your tribe and community about your book – through your list, social media and provide an incentive for people to share and promote it
- Follow the Amazon best-seller plan to get your book to number 1 on Amazon
- Create a website purely for your book so that people have a central place to find out more (and to buy it)
- Get someone famous or influential in your field to write the foreword for you
- Ask people to give you testimonials and ask

them to put the reviews onto Amazon
- Use online book clubs like www.Goodreads. com to help you to promote your book
- Do guest blogs, share snippets with your target clients and get them excited about your book
- Sell your book when you speak at networking groups and conferences
- Contact your local paper, magazines, radio, and TV for some great publicity or get some PR support

Getting help with your book

As I mentioned at the beginning of this chapter, writing a book is not going to make you millions – or at least your first book won't anyway – but writing your book will give you the expert status and shows that you have made the decision to stand out from the crowd. How many people are just thinking about writing a book rather than doing it? Or perhaps they have started their book, but not had the impetus behind finishing it. Are you one of these people?

If you think you might struggle, why not get a book coach or a mentor to help you or find a writing day or workshop that will help you to get started? Remember the journey of a thousand miles starts with the first step, so what is the first step you need to take to get your book on the road?

Chapter 12
Stand out in other ways

'As we let our light shine, we unconsciously give other
people permission to do the same.
As we are liberated from our own fear,
our presence actually liberates others.'
– *Marianne Williamson*

There are other ways in which you can stand out in
business, and I am going to talk about 5 of these.
They are winning awards, getting PR, running virtual
events, getting support, and leveraging your success.

Stand out by winning awards

Some solopreneurs decide to stand out by winning
awards. When I talk about awards, I mean business
awards, industry awards, mumpreneur awards and
the like, where you go through a process and get
nominated, shortlisted and, if you are lucky, win the
award.

If you choose to stand out by winning awards,
there are advantages to this process. You can raise
your profile, get great publicity, and perhaps win a
prize! You can also leverage your success by asking
your connections and clients to nominate you or vote
for you and help you to achieve the result you want.

There are a huge number of awards out there,
so start by finding out what awards are available and
their process, as the way in which they each work

will depend on the company organising the awards ceremony. For some awards, you will be able to self nominate and for others, you will rely on others to nominate you (although I'm sure you can put in a quiet word!) Some awards require nominations where the quality of your nomination and the size of your contact list is important. In others, you may have to justify your nomination through an application process, which may include an application form, video, and one-to-one meeting.

Like any process, if you want to win awards, make this part of your strategy, just like you would if you were writing a book. Please note, you won't be able to do all of these 'stand out' strategies as there are only so many hours in the day!

I've been nominated and shortlisted for 3 awards to date (although I've not won one at the time of writing), but even if you don't win, it will still propel you into the realms of stardom and raise awareness of both you and your business.

How do you win an award?

1. Find out what awards are in your area or nationally, and are suitable for you and your business
2. Get nominated or nominate yourself for a suitable award
3. Do a great application – shoot a video explaining why you should be nominated; complete an application form or whatever is required. Remember to share what makes you unique. It's about you, your story and what you give to your clients, whether this is a transformation, the product that helps them or the difference you make to them

4. Get publicity for it – whether you are successful or not, get publicity for your nomination. If nothing else, add it to your website, your auto signature, social media updates, your story and at best, contact your local press, radio or TV

Are you going to start to stand out by winning awards?

If yes, what do you need to do first?

Stand out by getting PR and media coverage

Another way to stand out is by getting PR and media coverage. When I say get PR, I don't mean putting your advert in the local parish magazine; I'm talking about getting positive publicity in local or national papers, radio, magazines and TV.

To get publicity, there normally has to be a story behind what you have to share. It's not enough (usually) to write a press release and then expect it to be published, unless you have a fantastic story behind the press release. PR can have a positive effect on your business, although not everyone knows how to achieve this easily.

I believe it is not about what you know but who you know, and having the right strategies in place bodes you well. You could choose to get PR by yourself (but is it the best use of your time?) or you could choose an expert to help you to become noticed.

If you are starting by yourself, here are a few tips: To get good PR, start by doing your research on what is read, watched or seen by your target market and then start to create relationships with the appropriate journalists. You may start with your local paper, or contact relevant magazines or perhaps your local radio station. Once you have started to build relationships, create a media list, which will include the contact details of the people you know about and may have already contacted. When you are ready, provide interesting content to the journalist. I hate to say this, but journalists are not interested in you – they are only interested in a story that sells. This may be your story, or your clients' stories (you will, of course, require permission in this instance).

I used to have a monthly slot on a local radio station (Express FM) where I shared my career tips for listeners. I've also been on Radio Solent and on Portsmouth Live TV three times (one of which was a couple of hours before my first book launch) and I have shared strategies around career change, confidence and business success. I have also had numerous articles published in the local paper, online and in national magazines.

Successes I have seen and suggested to clients include contacting journalists when a national or international event takes place, such as national stress awareness day, when you might propose an article to a journalist that relates to that day. If you think about it, it saves the journalist time in writing something that is relevant. Once journalists get to know you, they will also start to contact you when they believe you can help them out. That creates a greater possibility of having a regular column in a newspaper or magazine.

You can also use your contacts to find out how you can get great publicity. Who do you know who can help you?

One of the things I suggest to my clients is that they start to create a toolkit of tips, articles and information that they can share when they take a call from a journalist. Many will want a rapid reply and if you can either answer them on the spot or phone them back a little later, you will have a greater opportunity to feature in a newspaper or magazine. I have written hundreds of articles, tips, documents and snippets which have been featured in my newsletter, blogs and ezine articles, which enables me to pull out resources at a moment's notice. How can you do the same?

Think about your story or those of your clients that you can use either with their permission or confidentially. What story would be interesting to readers?

What is the next step you need to take?

Stand out by running virtual events

Since writing my first book, teleseminars and webinars are becoming much more mainstream. Most days I see a new virtual event being created and run by someone in my circle of influence. Yet, what I have noticed is that these are done by the minority rather than the majority. I have found virtual events to be a great way to build my list, share useful information, and develop an international community.

Earlier this year I ran a *Grow your Business with Teleseminars and Webinars* webinar with my clients which enabled them to learn more about the pros and cons and why this may be an important strategy for their business. Why don't I share a few of my tips with you about running virtual events?

6 advantages to running virtual events:

1. Flexibility – for both you and your clients and they can be run at a time to suit you. There is no need to go out, arrange childcare or travel arrangements, and there are no barriers to location – people can listen in and participate

across the world.
2. There is a shorter lead in time than promoting and running physical events. Typically, if you are promoting a virtual event, about 2-4 weeks is sufficient, whereas for a live event you need at least 6-8 weeks.
3. It is low cost for individuals and organisations and you can easily get everyone together in one place.
4. They can be profitable for businesses. You can run a free virtual event to lead clients to a paid programme, support a paid programme or you can use them as a showcase for your talents and expertise.
5. You can also sell them as a recorded product after the event and they can become a great product for your portfolio.
6. No one can see you (unless you use the webcam or you are with others!) so you don't need to dress up for the occasion.

When it comes to virtual events, I would love to say that they are always easy and seamless, but I would be lying! I've managed to mute myself, lose my interviewee and most recently, I had to abandon a webinar completely when the technology failed. That aside, they are a great way to leverage your knowledge and what you do, so keep in touch to find out when I'm running my next webinar.

I personally love the flexibility of virtual events. I'm an advocate of webinars, although for me, nothing quite matches the thrill of a live event (I can only share so much in this book!). Therefore, why not pop over to www.HowToStandOut.co.uk and I'll share a few more strategies and tips there and you can keep in touch too.

Stand out by getting support

When you make the decision to stand out, it is impossible to do everything by yourself. If you haven't learnt already, you will quickly find out that there are only so many hours in the day and days in the week to get things done. Get help from other experts to help you develop your business.

I am a great advocate of outsourcing. Get yourself a virtual assistant to help you with your admin; get a bookkeeper or an accountant to manage your books and file your accounts; get yourself a web designer to do your website; get a branding expert to help you with your message; get some PR support and get a coach or mentor to give you a kick up the backside! Need I go on?

I'm going to be controversial here. Many entrepreneurs, especially those running service-based businesses, decide to set up because of the low overheads. You can work from your spare room, set up a website cheaply, get a mobile and tell people you exist. However, unless you have a budget for marketing, PR, mentoring, you are going to struggle to stand out. If you try to do everything yourself, you will never have enough time and energy to provide a great service to your clients.

Every day I see coaches and other solopreneurs make huge and expensive mistakes, whether this is advertising that has failed to work, producing thousands of flyers with an unimpressive message, or spending time faffing around with something that doesn't make them money. Do you get the picture? If you are serious about being one of the 20% or fewer who make it in terms of running a successful business, you need to get help to make it happen. OK, rant over!

Stand out by leveraging what you do

With all of these strategies to stand out and shine, you need to learn how to leverage what you do. If you want to become the go-to-person in your area of expertise, find a way to inform people why you are this expert and learn how to raise your profile.

You may find that you need to start being opinionated if you are not naturally inclined to be that way. If you put a different, unique, or controversial slant on what you say or how you say it, you will certainly become noticed!

But what you will find when you raise your head above the parapet is that you are more likely to be noticed and get more clients. When you are one of many, there will be nothing that differentiates you from the crowd, and this is why I believe you need to find a way of standing out that works for you.

For more ways to stand out in your business, pop over to www.HowToStandOut.co.uk. Join our community, download our tips and share your strategies with others who share your passion and enthusiasm.

Chapter 13
What do you need to do next to stand out?

'Be yourself. Above all, let who you are, what you are, what you believe shine through every sentence you write, every piece you finish.' – *John Jakes*

I do hope that you have gained huge benefits from this book. I have imparted some of the secrets and strategies that I have learnt from some of the most successful coaches, mentors and experts in the industry and incorporated them into my business.

My aim in writing this book is to candidly share my stories, give you tips and strategies that you can apply yourself, and to tell you how you can do it. I want more people like you to have the confidence to take action, to dream big and make your goals happen.

As I said earlier and would like to reinforce, if you don't tell people that you exist, you won't be able to share your gifts, your knowledge, and your expertise with your clients. You have to stand up and be counted – be different, unique, or memorable – to achieve success. You have to have something that people want rather than what you think they want.

You have to ignite your passion, feel congruent with your message and do what it takes to make it happen. You have to be willing to become noticed, so that people know you exist, know who you are and know what you do. You also need to elevate your expertise so people recognise you as the expert in your field.

What is the difference that makes the difference?

I've talked about my SUCCESS system and have gone into more detail in this book, and I've talked about standing out from the crowd, but what is the difference that makes the difference in terms of business success?

Standing out strategies

- Model people who are expert at what you want to do – if I had not done this, my business would not be alive and thriving today nor would I be helping you to stand out in your business
- Do the 'stand out' thing that works for you. There's not much point in forcing the issue and being a gibbering wreck on stage or spending ages staring at a blank screen when you feel you *should* be writing
- Spend time with people who inspire you, who motivate you and who get you excited
- Never stop learning – from the latest updates in your profession, to new techy tips, to business strategies that work. Always learn, discount what you don't need to know, and discover what the experts are talking about
- Get yourself a coach or mentor – even if you don't know how you are going to fund it. The best mentors will help you to recoup your investment by sharing the strategies that work and stop you wasting money on the stuff that doesn't get you results
- Remember to do what you love and love what you do, then work won't seem like work and you'll reap the rewards of doing it

- Always focus on your bigger vision and how you are going to get there. If you want to live abroad, working on your laptop, what is stopping you?

So what's next? How are you going to stand out, step up and shine?

Keep in touch and share the strategies that you use to stand out like a star and shine. Remember to register at www.HowToStandOut.co.uk. Join our community, download our tips and spend time with others just like you!

About Karen Williams

Karen Williams is regarded as the *Coaches' Secret Weapon*. She works with coaches and solopreneurs to get great results in their business.

For Karen, it was not always easy. Like many coaches, she trained to become a coach when she experienced being coached. Stuck in a rut at work, Karen found her very first coach on Ebay and was inspired to train as a coach herself.

She qualified as a coach in 2006 and one of the things she noticed is that there are many great coaches, but many struggled to be successful in terms running a business. In this field, statistics indicate that just 10% of coaches make it. What was apparent was that many made it to the end of their qualification but failed to realise that this was just the start of their journey, and that they needed to learn so many more new skills to make it in business.

How does she know? At that time, she was one of them! Karen thought it would be easy – have 1000 glossy brochures printed, order some business cards, and set up a website. She thought she would go along to networking events and people would be clamouring for her services, but boy was she wrong!

Therefore, she had 2 options: option 1 was to stay in the corporate world, and option 2 was follow her heart into something she knew she loved. No marks for guessing which option she took! That's why, over the last two years she has interviewed and learnt the secrets from 24 top performance coaches and numerous other solopreneurs. Although not part of her original plan, she now helps others to develop the business skills and confidence to create a successful business on their terms.

Karen's true passion is working with coaches, other 'people-helpers,' and solopreneurs to help them to be more successful. Doing it this way, she can help more people to live a happier and fulfilled life than she can by operating alone. She also knows that setting up a business is much easier when you know how, when you learn from the experts and discover the shortcuts to turn your business dreams into reality.

It is her 7 step SUCCESS system that allows her to easily and effortlessly share her expertise with her clients across the world, and give them the cutting-edge strategies and motivation to develop successful and profitable businesses.

Karen has spent 15 years in the corporate world – in management, training and Human Resources and therefore understands what organisations and individuals want and can help her clients to tap into that knowledge.

She has embraced the fact that to be successful you need to stand out, be a role model for others and take calculated risks along the way. This is the second of two published books to date. She is frequently invited to speak at events and conferences, has been nominated for numerous awards, and is often featured in the media.

Find out more about Karen and her work at:

www.SelfDiscoveryCoaching.co.uk
www.TheSecretsOfSuccessfulCoaches.com and
www.HowToStandOut.co.uk feature details of her two books available on Amazon. You can also follow Karen on

Facebook at www.facebook.com/selfdiscoverycoaching and Twitter as @selfdiscovery.

Alternatively, why not cut out the middle man, take some purposeful action and contact Karen for a free success discovery call and have a chat.

Lightning Source UK Ltd.
Milton Keynes UK
UKOW030611020513

210066UK00007B/138/P